Docker Simplified

Containerization for Beginners and Professionals

THOMPSON CARTER

Table of Content

TABLE OF CONTENTS

INTRODUCTION

Welcome to *Docker Simplified: Containerization for Beginners and Professionals*. This book is designed to demystify Docker and containerization technology for readers at all levels—whether you're just starting out or looking to deepen your expertise. In today's fast-paced digital landscape, the ability to package, deploy, and scale applications efficiently is more critical than ever. Docker has emerged as a transformative technology that not only streamlines development but also revolutionizes how applications are built and managed across diverse environments.

Why Containerization Matters

Traditional methods of deploying applications—often based on monolithic architectures and physical or virtual machines—can be slow, inflexible, and resource-intensive. Containerization offers a modern solution by encapsulating applications and their dependencies into lightweight, portable units that run consistently across any environment. This technology eliminates the notorious "it works on my machine" problem, ensuring that what you develop locally behaves the same way in testing, staging, and production. With Docker leading the charge, containerization has become a cornerstone of modern DevOps practices, microservices architectures, and cloud-native applications.

Who Should Read This Book

This book is for everyone who wants to harness the power of Docker, from beginners with little to no experience with containerization to seasoned professionals looking for advanced insights and real-world case studies. If you're a developer, IT administrator, DevOps engineer, or even a decision-maker aiming to understand how containerization can drive efficiency and innovation in your organization, you will find valuable, actionable content within these pages.

How the Book Is Structured

Docker Simplified is organized into six comprehensive parts, each building on the previous sections to provide a complete understanding of containerization technology:

- **Part I: Foundations of Containerization and Docker**
  Here, you will learn the evolution of virtual computing—from physical servers to virtual machines, and finally to containers. We introduce core Docker concepts such as images, containers, and the Docker Engine through straightforward explanations and real-world examples.
- **Part II: Deep Diving into Docker's Core Components**
  This section takes a closer look at essential building blocks like Dockerfiles, image creation, and container management. You'll discover best practices for writing efficient Dockerfiles, managing images, and understanding the container lifecycle, all while focusing on performance, security, and maintainability.
- **Part III: Scaling and Orchestration**
  As your applications grow, managing multiple containers becomes a challenge. This part covers orchestration platforms like Docker Compose, Docker Swarm, and Kubernetes. You will learn how to deploy multi-container applications, scale

services, and manage dynamic environments with automated load balancing and continuous deployment strategies.

- **Part IV: Security, Performance, and Reliability**
Security is paramount in any deployment. In this section, we delve into container security fundamentals and advanced measures, including vulnerability scanning, best practices for running non-root containers, compliance for regulated industries, and performance tuning. Real-world examples illustrate how to achieve high availability and disaster recovery in containerized systems.

- **Part V: Real-World Implementations and Use Cases**
Theory comes to life in this part with case studies from various industries such as finance, healthcare, media, and e-commerce. You'll see how enterprises have successfully adopted Docker to modernize legacy applications, build microservices architectures, and integrate with CI/CD pipelines. These examples provide practical insights and lessons learned from real deployments.

- **Part VI: Advanced Topics and Looking Ahead**
In our final section, we explore advanced topics and the future of container technology. We discuss monitoring and logging, the broader Docker ecosystem, third-party tools, and predictions for emerging trends such as serverless computing, edge computing, and evolving container standards. We conclude by forecasting Docker's expanding role in DevOps and its potential impact on emerging fields like AI and IoT.

What You Will Gain

By the end of this book, you will have:

- A solid understanding of Docker's core concepts and containerization principles.
- Practical experience with building, deploying, and managing Docker containers.
- Insights into container orchestration and scaling using tools like Docker Compose, Swarm, and Kubernetes.
- Knowledge of advanced security, performance tuning, and high availability strategies.
- Real-world examples and case studies that illustrate how Docker is transforming enterprise IT environments.
- A forward-looking perspective on how emerging trends will shape the future of containerization and DevOps.

Whether you're setting up your first container or architecting a complex microservices platform, this book provides the knowledge and practical tools you need to succeed in a containerized world. Let's embark on this journey to unlock the full potential of Docker and transform how you build, deploy, and manage applications.

Welcome to the future of containerization!

PART I

Foundations of Containerization and Docker

CHAPTER 1

From Virtual Machines to Containers

Introduction

For decades, organizations and developers have sought better ways to run their software applications. Early on, we relied on physical machines—each server dedicated to running specific tasks. Over time, as the demands of software grew, we needed more efficient methods to use these servers. This need led to virtual machines, a concept that revolutionized the way we think about deploying, managing, and isolating different applications on shared hardware.

But while virtual machines solved many problems, they also introduced a set of new ones: high overhead, large disk images, and complexity in setup and maintenance. Enter **containerization**—a leaner, more flexible approach that gives developers and system administrators the ability to package applications and their dependencies into lightweight units called **containers**. Containers allow you to run multiple apps on the same machine with minimal overhead and better resource sharing.

In this chapter, we'll explore the transition from physical servers to virtual machines, then from virtual machines to containers. We'll discuss why virtual machines were a huge step forward, where they fell short, and how containers address these challenges. By the end, you'll understand the basic differences between virtual machines and containers, and why containerization (with Docker at the forefront) has reshaped modern application deployment.

1.1 The Historical Context of Server Virtualization

1.1.1 The Early Days: Physical Servers

Before virtualization became mainstream, organizations typically dedicated entire physical servers to specific purposes. For example, a company might have:

- **Mail Server**: Handling all incoming and outgoing emails.
- **Web Server**: Hosting the company's website or internal applications.
- **Database Server**: Managing the organization's structured data.

This setup often led to under-utilized servers. A single machine might be working at only 10% of its capacity most of the time, but it still consumed the same amount of electricity, cooling, and floor space. The biggest downside was that if a department needed a new application, the organization often had to purchase another physical server, which was expensive and time-consuming.

1.1.2 The Advent of Virtualization

Virtualization technology offered a solution by allowing multiple **virtual machines** (VMs) to run on a single physical machine. Each virtual machine acts like a complete computer with its own operating system (OS), memory, CPU, and storage. This is achieved by a piece of software known as a **hypervisor** (e.g., VMware ESXi, Microsoft Hyper-V, or open-source solutions like KVM).

Key benefits of virtualization included:

1. **Server Consolidation**: Instead of each application needing its own physical server, multiple virtual machines could share one powerful physical server.
2. **Isolation**: Each VM was separated from the others; a crash or security issue in one VM typically didn't affect the others running on the same host.
3. **Flexibility**: Businesses could spin up or shut down VMs as needed, improving resource efficiency.

Virtualization drastically reduced hardware costs and improved resource utilization. It also paved the way for modern cloud computing platforms—like Amazon Web Services (AWS), Microsoft Azure, and Google Cloud—which rely heavily on virtual machine technology to power their services.

1.2 Key Limitations of Virtual Machines

Despite the immense benefits, virtual machines aren't perfect. Some of their common limitations include:

1.2.1 Resource Overhead

Each virtual machine runs its own full-fledged operating system. That means if you have four VMs on one physical server, you essentially have four separate operating systems running. Even if these VMs only host small applications, each VM needs system libraries, background services, a kernel (the OS's core), and so on. This redundancy leads to substantial overhead in terms of memory, CPU consumption, and disk space.

1.2.2 Slower Boot and Deployment Times

Spinning up a new VM can be slower compared to starting a lightweight process. A VM typically goes through a boot sequence similar to a physical machine, loading the operating system from scratch. For an enterprise environment, this might not be a deal-breaker, but in a fast-paced DevOps pipeline—where you want to make frequent updates or test new builds quickly—VM boot times can become a bottleneck.

1.2.3 Complexity in Maintenance

Maintaining multiple operating systems (patching, updating security policies, installing drivers, etc.) is more involved when each VM is its own environment. Although automation tools exist, every new VM typically needs separate attention.

1.2.4 Inefficient Use of Resources

If you only need to run a small service, deploying it on a full-blown VM can be wasteful. You'll be dedicating an entire guest operating system's worth of RAM and CPU, even if the app itself only requires a fraction of those resources.

These pain points nudged engineers to look for a more efficient way to run applications without the bulk of a separate operating system for each instance. That's where containerization stepped in.

1.3 The Emergence of Containerization

1.3.1 Roots in Unix Chroot

Container-like features existed in various forms for decades. A feature known as **chroot** in Unix-based systems (introduced as early as 1979) allowed administrators to isolate a process by changing its file system root directory. This setup provided some basic isolation, but it wasn't as robust or user-friendly as modern containers.

1.3.2 Linux Containers (LXC) and Beyond

Fast forward to the 2000s, and the Linux community began incorporating kernel features like **cgroups** (control groups) and **namespaces**. These features gave processes their own isolated environment, limiting access to system resources such as CPU time, memory, network stacks, and file systems. By combining these kernel features, Linux distributions enabled the creation of **LXC (Linux Containers)**, an early container implementation.

1.3.3 Docker's Breakthrough

While LXC was powerful, it required considerable expertise to set up and manage. In 2013, a company named **dotCloud** (later renamed Docker, Inc.) introduced Docker. Docker built on top of these Linux kernel capabilities but wrapped them in a straightforward interface and automated many of the cumbersome steps. This breakthrough made containerization accessible to mainstream developers and organizations.

Key reasons Docker took off:

- **Ease of Use**: Docker provided a simple command-line interface (CLI) and a descriptive file (called a Dockerfile) to automate the creation of containers.
- **Standardization**: Docker introduced a standard image format, enabling people to share and deploy containers consistently.
- **Ecosystem and Community**: Early adoption by major tech companies and open-source enthusiasts propelled Docker to the forefront of containerization solutions.

1.4 How Containers Differ from VMs

The fundamental difference between containers and virtual machines lies in their approach to **isolation** and **resource usage**.

1.4.1 Operating System Sharing

- **Virtual Machines**: Each VM includes a **full guest operating system** on top of a hypervisor.
- **Containers**: Multiple containers share the **host's operating system kernel**. Each container runs as an isolated process with its own filesystem, CPU, memory, and network stack, but they still rely on the underlying OS for core services.

Because containers share the host operating system kernel, they avoid the overhead of starting and running multiple full-fledged operating systems. This design dramatically **reduces memory** and **CPU overhead**, allowing for faster startup times and better resource utilization.

1.4.2 Size and Efficiency

- **Virtual Machines**: VM images can be several gigabytes in size because they often contain an entire operating system, plus installed libraries, frameworks, and the application itself.

- **Containers**: Container images are typically smaller. They may start with a minimal base image (like Alpine Linux, which is only a few megabytes), then layer on only what the application needs.

This difference in size and resource use means you can often run **dozens** or even **hundreds** of containers on a machine that could only realistically handle a handful of virtual machines.

1.4.3 Isolation and Security

- **Virtual Machines**: Because each VM includes an entire OS, the isolation boundary is **very strong**. However, a bug in the hypervisor or misconfiguration could still affect security across VMs.
- **Containers**: Containers rely on the kernel's namespaces and cgroups. They're secure enough for many use cases, but they share the kernel with the host, so if the kernel is compromised, it could affect all containers.

In practice, containers are considered sufficiently secure for a broad spectrum of applications. Enterprises handle sensitive workloads in containers every day, using additional security measures (like container scanning, user namespacing, SELinux, AppArmor, etc.) to further reduce risk.

1.4.4 Use Cases

- **Virtual Machines**:
  - Running different operating systems on the same hardware (e.g., Windows, Linux, or older OS versions).

- o Consolidating servers in a data center environment.
- o Providing robust isolation at scale (often important in multi-tenant cloud environments).
- **Containers**:
  - o Microservices-based applications where each service runs in its own container.
  - o Continuous Integration/Continuous Deployment (CI/CD) pipelines requiring fast creation and teardown of environments.
  - o Quickly setting up consistent development environments, ensuring "it works on my machine" truly translates to production.

1.5 Real-World Example: Moving from a VM-Based Solution to Docker

To illustrate the benefits of containers, let's look at a small-scale, real-world scenario. Suppose you have a modest web application—let's call it **AppX**—written in Node.js, connected to a PostgreSQL database. You've been running AppX on a **virtual machine** hosted on a cloud provider. The VM setup might look like this:

- **Operating System**: Ubuntu 20.04 (Guest OS)
- **Node.js & AppX**: Node.js installed system-wide, along with your application code.
- **PostgreSQL**: Installed within the same VM.
- **Physical Host**: Provided by the cloud vendor, running a hypervisor that hosts your VM.

1.5.1 The VM Approach

1. You spin up a cloud VM with 2 CPUs and 4GB of RAM.
2. You install Ubuntu, run system updates, install Node.js, and configure PostgreSQL.

3. You deploy AppX by pulling the code from a repository, installing dependencies, and starting the service.
4. The database, web server, and application server all run inside the same virtual machine.

This method works, but it has drawbacks:

- **Overhead**: Ubuntu plus the virtualization overhead consumes a chunk of your 4GB RAM allocation. The hypervisor itself also adds overhead.
- **Lack of Modularity**: The database and application are on the same VM. If you need to scale AppX by adding more instances, you might deploy another entire VM or upgrade to a bigger instance.
- **Maintenance**: Patching Ubuntu and upgrading Node.js or PostgreSQL require repeated manual steps. If something breaks, it might require a system rollback or re-imaging the VM.

1.5.2 Transition to Docker Containers

Now, let's see how Docker can improve this setup.

1. **Install Docker on the Host Machine**: Instead of spinning up a dedicated virtual machine for everything, you might either:
   o Use a smaller VM that only has Docker installed, or
   o Run Docker on a cloud container service that abstracts away the OS.
2. **Create Separate Containers**:
   o **AppX Container**: A Docker container based on a lightweight Node.js image. This container runs only the application code.
   o **PostgreSQL Container**: A Docker container from an official PostgreSQL image, storing its data in a **Docker volume** (so the data persists even if the container restarts).

40

3. **Network and Deployment**:
   - Use Docker's built-in networking to allow the AppX container to talk to the PostgreSQL container internally.
   - Expose only the necessary ports (e.g., port 80 or 443 for the web) to the outside world for security.
4. **Resource Efficiency**:
   - Both containers share the host's (or VM's) operating system kernel.
   - Each container includes only the binaries and libraries necessary for Node.js or PostgreSQL. There's no need for a full operating system in each container.
5. **Scalability**:
   - If AppX experiences heavier traffic, you can quickly spin up multiple replicas of the AppX container, all communicating with the same database container or a replicated setup.
   - No need to provision a full new VM or re-install the OS and dependencies each time.
6. **Simplified Maintenance**:
   - Updating Node.js or PostgreSQL is as simple as pulling a new Docker image and recreating the containers.
   - If something goes wrong, rolling back to a previous version is much simpler: just revert to the older container image.

1.5.3 Resource Savings in Numbers

Let's assume:

- The original VM used 1GB of RAM for the OS, background services, and overhead, leaving only 3GB for Node.js and PostgreSQL.
- The containerized setup runs with minimal overhead. The Node.js container might consume 500MB of RAM when under typical load, and PostgreSQL might consume 1GB.

41

This leaves even more space for additional containers or other processes.

Furthermore, the CPU overhead in the containerized setup is typically lower than in a VM-based setup because you aren't running multiple kernels. The result is that on the same physical hardware, you can often run many more containerized applications than you could with VM-based ones.

Conclusion

Virtual machines revolutionized application deployment by allowing multiple OS environments to coexist on the same hardware. However, they also come with inherent overhead and complexity. Containers build upon the isolation principles of virtualization but use **process-level isolation** rather than requiring separate operating systems for each instance. This approach leads to faster start times, more efficient resource use, and a simpler model for creating, distributing, and running applications.

Understanding the historical context of server virtualization helps you appreciate why Docker (and containers in general) have become such a game-changer. Containers solve the overhead issues of VMs for many scenarios, while still providing the isolation needed for modern application deployment, especially in microservices architectures and DevOps workflows.

As you move forward in this book, you'll learn how to install Docker, work with images and containers, and eventually move on to orchestrating entire fleets of containers. You'll gain insight into security best practices, performance tuning, and real-world use cases that will help you deploy applications more effectively—whether you're migrating a small, single-server app or scaling up a complex, distributed system.

In the next chapter, **Chapter 2: Understanding Docker at a High Level**, we'll build on what you've learned here by exploring Docker's core components—images, containers, and the Docker Engine—and how they fit into modern software development. We'll also look at how Docker is changing the way teams collaborate on code and infrastructure.

Key Takeaways

- **Virtual Machines** vs. **Containers**: VMs package up entire operating systems, whereas containers share the underlying host OS kernel and are more lightweight.
- **Main Advantages of Containers**: Lower overhead, faster startup times, easier maintenance, and more efficient use of resources.
- **Historical Context**: Virtualization was a huge leap forward, but the overhead led to innovations like Docker, which leverages Linux kernel features for a more lightweight approach.
- **Real-World Impact**: By transitioning from a VM-based setup to containers, organizations can save on resources, gain flexibility, and streamline updates and deployments.

CHAPTER 2

Understanding Docker ata High Level

Introduction

In the previous chapter, we explored the historical journey from physical servers to virtual machines, and ultimately, how containerization emerged to offer a more efficient alternative. Now, we'll focus specifically on Docker—arguably the most popular containerization platform in use today.

By the end of this chapter, you'll have a solid grasp of Docker's fundamental concepts: **images**, **containers**, and the **Docker Engine**. We'll see where Docker fits into modern software development practices, discover its application across various industries, and walk through a simple "Hello, World" project to illustrate the workflow in action.

2.1 What Is Docker?

At its core, **Docker** is a platform that enables you to package applications and their dependencies into isolated environments called **containers**. These containers share the host's operating system but remain separated from each other—each container has its own filesystem, memory, network stack, and processes, yet they're more lightweight than virtual machines.

When you hear "Docker," people might be referring to several related components:

1. **Docker Engine**: The runtime that builds and runs containers.
2. **Docker CLI** (Command-Line Interface): The primary tool developers and sysadmins use to interact with Docker (e.g., `docker run`, `docker build`).
3. **Docker Hub**: A public registry of images that anyone can pull and run, as well as a place to store and share your own images.

Why Does Docker Matter?

- **Consistency**: Docker ensures that your application runs the same way regardless of the environment—be it your local machine, a test server, or a production data center.
- **Efficiency**: Containers start up faster and use fewer resources compared to full-blown virtual machines.
- **Portability**: A Docker container packaged on a laptop can be deployed to a cloud server with minimal tweaks, simplifying the process of moving applications between different environments.

2.2 Core Concepts: Images, Containers, and the Docker Engine

2.2.1 Docker Engine

Docker Engine is the beating heart of Docker. It's a service (or daemon) running in the background on your system. When you execute commands like `docker run hello-`

`world`, the Docker CLI communicates with the Docker Engine, which then does the heavy lifting of:

- Pulling images from a registry (like Docker Hub)
- Creating and starting containers
- Managing resources like storage, memory, network, and CPU

You can think of the Docker Engine as a virtual shipyard manager: it builds, launches, and oversees all your container "ships."

2.2.2 Docker Images

A **Docker image** is a read-only template that contains the application code, runtime, libraries, environment variables, and configuration files needed to run a container. Images are built layer by layer, using a specification file called a **Dockerfile**.

For example, you might have a Docker image based on a minimal Linux distribution (like **Alpine**). On top of that base layer, you install Node.js, add your application files, and define how they run. This layered approach saves disk space—if two images share some layers, Docker only stores those shared layers once.

Key Points About Images:

- **Immutable**: Images don't change once they're created. If you need a new version, you build a new image.
- **Versioned**: Images are typically **tagged** (e.g., `myapp:v1.0`, `myapp:latest`) to differentiate versions.
- **Sharable**: You can push images to registries like Docker Hub or a private registry, allowing others to pull them and run the same environment.

46

2.2.3 Docker Containers

When you run an image, you create a **container**—a running instance of that image with its own processes, memory, and network interface. Containers are ephemeral; you can start them, stop them, and remove them without affecting the original image. You can also run multiple containers from the same image simultaneously.

Key Points About Containers:

- **Isolated**: Each container operates in a sandboxed environment, using Linux kernel features like cgroups and namespaces for isolation.
- **Lightweight**: Containers share the host operating system's kernel, avoiding the overhead of separate OS installations.
- **Ephemeral**: Data stored inside a container disappears when the container is removed. For persistent storage, you can use Docker **volumes** or external storage solutions.

2.3 Where Docker Fits in Modern Software Development

Docker has become an integral part of contemporary development and DevOps workflows. Here's where it excels:

1. **Development Environments**
   o **Consistency**: A developer can ensure everyone on the team uses the same development environment. No more "it works on my machine" issues.

- o **Easy Setup**: Installing all dependencies within a Docker container means you don't have to clutter your host machine.
- o **Rapid Prototyping**: Need a specific version of Python or Node.js for a quick test? Pull a container image for it, run it, and discard it when you're done.

2. **Continuous Integration/Continuous Deployment (CI/CD)**
    - o **Automated Builds**: CI tools like Jenkins, GitLab, or GitHub Actions can build new Docker images whenever code changes, ensuring consistency.
    - o **Automated Tests**: Tests can run in a containerized environment that mirrors production, catching issues early.
    - o **Seamless Deployments**: Once an image passes all tests, it's promoted to production. Rolling back means simply redeploying a previous image.

3. **Microservices Architectures**
    - o **Service Isolation**: Each microservice runs in its own container, making it easier to update or scale each service independently.
    - o **Composable**: Tools like Docker Compose or Kubernetes manage how individual containers communicate.
    - o **Scalability**: Spin up more containers for high-traffic services without impacting the rest of the system.

4. **Cloud-Native Deployments**
    - o **Portability**: Container images can run on any cloud platform supporting Docker (e.g., AWS, Azure, GCP).
    - o **Serverless and Beyond**: Many serverless frameworks and Functions-as-a-Service offerings either use containers under the hood or allow you to deploy Docker images directly.

48

o **Hybrid Approaches**: You can mix and match on-premises servers with public cloud container services, maintaining a consistent Docker-based workflow.

2.4 Introductory Use Cases Across Different Industries

Docker isn't just for web developers. It's applicable in nearly every industry that relies on software:

1. **Web Development**
   o Host environments for content management systems (CMS) like WordPress or Drupal in reproducible Docker containers.
   o Keep backend and frontend stacks isolated to avoid conflicting dependencies.
2. **Data Science & Machine Learning**
   o Package Jupyter notebooks along with Python libraries (NumPy, pandas, TensorFlow, etc.) in a single container.
   o Ensure reproducible experiments by controlling library versions and data dependencies.
   o Easily deploy machine learning models to production without rewriting the environment setup.
3. **Financial Services**
   o Rapidly provision test environments that mirror complex production setups, including multiple microservices and databases.
   o Enhance security by isolating sensitive components (e.g., payment processing) in dedicated containers.
4. **Healthcare**
   o Simplify compliance by deploying containerized applications with consistent configurations.

> o Scale patient data management solutions quickly while maintaining HIPAA-related security controls.

5. **Gaming and Media**
   > o Run game servers inside containers for efficient scaling, especially during peak usage.
   > o Transcode media files in containerized pipelines that can scale based on demand.

In essence, **any organization** looking for a consistent, portable way to deploy and manage software can benefit from Docker.

2.5 Real-World Example: Packaging a Simple "Hello, World" Node.js Application

Let's walk through a straightforward example of how Docker helps package an application. In this scenario, we'll create a tiny Node.js app that serves a "Hello, World" message and then containerize it.

2.5.1 Setting the Stage

Prerequisites:

- Docker installed on your machine (Linux, macOS, or Windows).
- Basic familiarity with Node.js (though the steps are simple and don't require deep knowledge).

The Application:

- A single file, app.js, that starts a Node.js server and returns "Hello, World" when you visit it in a browser.

Folder Structure:

```
hello-world-node/
 ├─ app.js
 └─ Dockerfile
```

2.5.2 Writing the Node.js Code (app.js)

```js
// app.js
const http = require('http');

const PORT = process.env.PORT || 3000;

const requestHandler = (req, res) => {
  res.end('Hello, World');
};

const                    server                   =
http.createServer(requestHandler);

server.listen(PORT, () => {
  console.log(`Server running on port ${PORT}`);
});
```

This script does three things:

1. Creates an HTTP server using Node.js.
2. Listens on port `3000` by default.
3. Sends a "Hello, World" response for every request.

2.5.3 Creating a Dockerfile

A **Dockerfile** tells Docker how to build an image. Here's a minimal example:

```dockerfile
```

51

```
# Use an official Node.js image as a base
FROM node:16-alpine

# Set the working directory inside the container
WORKDIR /usr/src/app

# Copy package.json and package-lock.json if you
have dependencies
# For a simple Hello, World, we might not need
them, but let's include the step for best
practice
COPY package*.json ./

# Install dependencies (if any)
RUN npm install

# Copy our application code
COPY . .

# Expose the port (informational; not strictly
required)
EXPOSE 3000

# Define the command to run our app
CMD ["node", "app.js"]
```

Explanation:

- **FROM node:16-alpine**: Specifies the base image—Node.js 16 on a lightweight Alpine Linux.
- **WORKDIR /usr/src/app**: All subsequent commands run in /usr/src/app inside the container.
- **COPY package*.json ./** and **RUN npm install**: Copy package files and install dependencies.
- **COPY . .**: Copies the rest of the application files into the container.
- **EXPOSE 3000**: Documents that the container listens on port 3000.
- **CMD ["node", "app.js"]**: Tells Docker how to start the Node.js server when the container runs.

2.5.4 Building and Running the Container

Step 1: Open your terminal or command prompt in the `hello-world-node/` directory and build the Docker image:

bash

```
docker build -t hello-world-node .
```

- **-t hello-world-node**: Assigns a name (tag) to the image.
- .: Tells Docker to look for the Dockerfile in the current directory.

Step 2: Verify that the image built successfully by listing your local images:

bash

```
docker images
```

You should see `hello-world-node` in the list.

Step 3: Run a container based on this image:

bash

```
docker run -d -p 3000:3000 --name my-hello-app hello-world-node
```

- **-d**: Runs the container in the background (detached).
- **-p 3000:3000**: Maps port 3000 on your host to port 3000 inside the container, so you can access the app via `http://localhost:3000`.
- **--name my-hello-app**: Assigns a custom name to the container for easier management.
- **hello-world-node**: Specifies the image name we want to run.

2.5.5 Testing the Application

Open your web browser and go to `http://localhost:3000`. You should see:

```
Hello, World
```

Check the container logs (optional):

```
bash

docker logs my-hello-app
```

You'll see a message confirming that the server started:

```
arduino

Server running on port 3000
```

Congratulations—you just built and ran a Docker container that serves a simple Node.js application!

2.5.6 Cleaning Up

When you're done, stop and remove the container:

```
bash

docker stop my-hello-app
docker rm my-hello-app
```

If you no longer need the image, you can also remove it:

```
bash

docker rmi hello-world-node
```

2.6 Why This Matters

This basic "Hello, World" container might seem small, but it demonstrates key Docker workflows:

1. **Image Creation**: You used a Dockerfile to define your environment and how to run your app.
2. **Port Mapping**: You exposed the container's port and mapped it to your machine, making the app accessible.
3. **Isolation**: The Node.js environment lives inside a container, separate from your host system's libraries and configurations.
4. **Reproducibility**: Anyone with Docker installed can run the exact same environment and application code—no setup conflicts, no messy "dependency hell."

The real power of Docker shines when you scale up. Imagine a microservice architecture with a dozen services—each one can be packaged as a container. When you're ready to test or deploy, you can spin up all those containers in a matter of seconds using tools like Docker Compose or orchestration platforms such as Kubernetes or Docker Swarm.

Conclusion

In this chapter, we explored what Docker is at a high level and why it matters so much in modern software development. We introduced Docker's core concepts— **images**, **containers**, and the **Docker Engine**—and covered real-world use cases spanning multiple industries, from web development to data science.

The "Hello, World" Node.js example demonstrated how straightforward it can be to package and run an application in a Docker container. Even a simple example highlights Docker's core strengths: **portability**, **consistency**, and **efficiency**.

Next up, we'll get more hands-on with installing and setting up Docker for various operating systems in **Chapter 3: Setting Up Your Docker Environment**. You'll learn how to verify that Docker is running correctly, handle common installation pitfalls, and gain a deeper understanding of the Docker CLI's essential commands.

Key Takeaways

- **Docker** is a containerization platform that packages applications into lightweight, isolated units called **containers**.
- **Docker Images** are read-only templates containing the application code, runtime, and dependencies. **Containers** are the running instances of those images.
- **Docker Engine** is the service that coordinates the building and running of containers on your host machine.
- **Use Cases** range from local development environments and CI/CD pipelines to microservices architectures and big data workloads across industries.
- **Real-World Example**: Packaging a Node.js "Hello, World" application in a Docker container highlights how easy it is to build, run, and share containerized applications.

CHAPTER 3

Setting Up Your Docker Environment

Introduction

So far, we've learned about containerization's evolution and Docker's core concepts. But you can't truly appreciate Docker's benefits until you set it up and run your first container. In this chapter, we'll walk you through installing Docker on **Windows**, **macOS**, and **Linux**. We'll also show how to verify your setup is correct by running a few test containers. Finally, we'll explore some of the most common troubleshooting tips to help you avoid getting stuck on Day One.

Whether you're a developer wanting to containerize your own apps, or a systems administrator tasked with managing a production environment, this chapter equips you with the knowledge to install Docker quickly and effectively. By the time you finish, you'll be ready to build and run containers in your own environment.

3.1 Installing Docker on Windows

3.1.1 System Requirements

- **Operating System**: Windows 10 (Professional or Enterprise) version 1904 or later, or Windows 11.

57

- **Hardware**: 64-bit system with at least 4GB of RAM.
- **Virtualization Enabled**: Ensure **Hyper-V** or **WSL 2** is enabled. Docker Desktop on Windows relies on these technologies for containerization.

Note: Windows 10 Home editions (older versions) require using **WSL 2** (Windows Subsystem for Linux) instead of Hyper-V. Most modern Windows editions now support WSL 2.

3.1.2 Downloading Docker Desktop for Windows

1. **Visit Docker's Official Website**: Go to Docker's download page.
2. **Select Docker Desktop for Windows**: Download the installer (.exe file).
3. **Run the Installer**: Follow the prompts. When prompted, you can choose between using Hyper-V or WSL 2 as your backend. If you're unsure, WSL 2 generally offers better performance and compatibility.

3.1.3 Post-Installation Setup

After installation completes:

1. **Launch Docker Desktop**: The Docker whale icon appears in your system tray.
2. **Initial Configuration**: Docker Desktop might prompt you to enable Hyper-V or WSL 2 if not already configured. Follow the on-screen instructions.
3. **Verify Docker Version**: Open **PowerShell** or **Command Prompt** and run:

```bash
docker version
```

You should see client and server versions listed, confirming Docker is installed and running.

3.2 Installing Docker on macOS

3.2.1 System Requirements

- **Operating System**: macOS 10.15 (Catalina) or later.
- **Hardware**: A 64-bit system with at least 4GB of RAM. Apple Silicon (M1, M2) is also supported by Docker Desktop for Mac, though you'll want to ensure you download the appropriate build.

3.2.2 Downloading Docker Desktop for Mac

1. **Visit Docker's Official Website**: Head to Docker's download page.
2. **Select Docker Desktop for Mac**: Choose the version matching your Mac's processor (Intel or Apple Silicon).
3. **Install**: Open the downloaded .dmg file and drag the Docker icon to your Applications folder.

3.2.3 Running Docker Desktop

1. **Launch Docker Desktop**: Open Docker Desktop from your Applications folder.
2. **Grant Permissions**: The first time you launch, macOS may prompt you to authorize system extensions. Click **Allow** if prompted.
3. **Verify Installation**: Open the **Terminal** app and run:

```bash
docker version
```

You should see Docker's client and server versions, indicating everything is up and running.

Tip: On Apple Silicon Macs, some Docker images may still be optimized for Intel chips. Docker handles this with emulation, but you might see performance differences compared to native ARM-based images.

3.3 Installing Docker on Linux

3.3.1 Supported Distributions

Docker provides packages for most popular Linux distributions, including:

- Ubuntu (LTS versions recommended)
- Debian
- Fedora
- CentOS
- openSUSE
- And many others (via community support)

3.3.2 Installing on Ubuntu (Example)

Let's use **Ubuntu** as our example. The steps are similar for other distributions, with minor command differences:

1. **Uninstall Old Docker Versions** (Optional)

   bash

   ```
   sudo apt-get remove docker docker-engine
   docker.io containerd runc
   ```

2. **Update Package Index**

```bash
sudo apt-get update
```

3. Install Dependencies

```bash
sudo apt-get install ca-certificates curl
gnupg lsb-release
```

4. Add Docker's Official GPG Key

```bash
curl                          -fsSL
https://download.docker.com/linux/ubuntu/
gpg    |    sudo    gpg    --dearmor    -o
/usr/share/keyrings/docker-archive-
keyring.gpg
```

5. Set Up the Stable Repository

```bash
echo \
  "deb [arch=$(dpkg --print-architecture)
signed-by=/usr/share/keyrings/docker-
archive-keyring.gpg]
https://download.docker.com/linux/ubuntu \
  $(lsb_release -cs) stable" | sudo tee
/etc/apt/sources.list.d/docker.list    >
/dev/null
```

6. Install Docker Engine

```bash
sudo apt-get update
sudo apt-get install docker-ce docker-ce-
cli containerd.io
```

7. **Check Docker Status**

```bash
sudo systemctl status docker
```

Ensure Docker is running. If necessary, enable it to start on boot:

```bash
sudo systemctl enable docker
```

8. **Run Docker Without sudo** (Optional)

```bash
sudo usermod -aG docker $USER
```

After running this, log out and log back in so your group membership is re-evaluated.

3.3.3 Verifying Installation on Linux

Open a terminal and run:

```bash
docker version
```

You should see the installed version details for both **client** and **server**. Next, test Docker by pulling a simple image:

```bash
docker run hello-world
```

If everything works, you'll see a welcome message from Docker.

3.4 Verifying a Successful Installation (All Platforms)

Once Docker is installed on Windows, macOS, or Linux, you can confirm it's functional by running the following **test container**:

bash

```
docker run hello-world
```

What Happens?

1. **Docker checks if "hello-world" exists** on your local machine.
2. If not, it pulls the "hello-world" image from Docker Hub (the default registry).
3. Docker creates and starts a container from that image.
4. The container prints a short message to your terminal, then exits.

A successful run confirms that:

- Your Docker Engine can communicate with Docker Hub.
- Your environment is correctly configured to pull images, create containers, and capture container output.

3.5 Basic Troubleshooting

Even though Docker aims to simplify application deployment, installation issues can arise. Here are some common pitfalls and quick fixes:

1. **Virtualization Disabled** (Windows/Mac)
   - o Make sure **virtualization** is enabled in your BIOS/UEFI settings (often labeled as "Intel VT-x" or "AMD-V").
   - o On Windows, verify **Hyper-V** or **WSL 2** is installed and active.
2. **Permissions Errors** (Linux)
   - o If you see messages like "permission denied" when running `docker` commands, add your user to the `docker` group and re-log.
   - o Verify Docker is running (`sudo systemctl status docker`).
3. **Conflict with Other Services**
   - o Sometimes leftover virtualization software or old Docker installations can interfere. Remove or disable conflicting services.
4. **Firewall or Proxy Issues**
   - o In corporate environments, firewalls or proxy settings can block Docker from pulling images. Configure Docker with your proxy settings if necessary.
5. **Incompatible OS Version**
   - o Ensure you're on a **supported** version of Windows, macOS, or Linux. Outdated OS versions may lack kernel features required by Docker.

Finding More Help

Docker's official documentation and community forums are excellent resources. If you're stuck, searching for your error message often leads to solutions that have worked for others.

3.6 Real-World Example: Installing Docker on a Fresh Cloud VM

Containers are especially common in cloud environments, where you can quickly spin up a server and deploy Dockerized apps. Let's walk through installing Docker on a fresh Ubuntu VM in the cloud. The steps are similar for other Linux distributions.

3.6.1 Setting Up an Ubuntu VM

Step 1: Choose Your Cloud Provider Popular providers include **AWS**, **DigitalOcean**, **Google Cloud**, **Azure**, etc. Let's say you pick **AWS**.

Step 2: Create an EC2 Instance

- Log in to your AWS console, go to **EC2**, and click **Launch Instance**.
- Select the **Ubuntu** AMI (Amazon Machine Image).
- Choose an instance type (e.g., t2.micro or t3.micro) sufficient to test Docker.
- Configure security groups to allow SSH (port 22) and any other ports you might need later.

Step 3: Connect via SSH

- Once the instance is up, note the public IP or DNS name.
- SSH into the instance using your key pair:

```bash
ssh -i /path/to/your-key.pem ubuntu@ec2-xx-xx-xx-xx.compute-1.amazonaws.com
```

3.6.2 Installing Docker on the VM

Once you're connected to the server, follow the **Linux installation steps** (shown earlier for Ubuntu) to add Docker's GPG key, repository, and install Docker Engine.

For instance:

bash

```
# Uninstall any old Docker packages
sudo apt-get remove docker docker-engine
docker.io containerd runc

# Update package list
sudo apt-get update

# Install packages to allow apt to use a
repository over HTTPS
sudo apt-get install ca-certificates curl gnupg
lsb-release

# Add Docker's official GPG key
curl                              -fsSL
https://download.docker.com/linux/ubuntu/gpg   |
sudo         gpg         --dearmor        -o
/usr/share/keyrings/docker-archive-keyring.gpg

# Add Docker's stable repository
echo \
  "deb    [arch=$(dpkg   --print-architecture)
signed-by=/usr/share/keyrings/docker-archive-
keyring.gpg]
https://download.docker.com/linux/ubuntu \
  $(lsb_release  -cs)  stable"  |  sudo  tee
/etc/apt/sources.list.d/docker.list > /dev/null

# Install Docker Engine
sudo apt-get update
sudo apt-get install docker-ce docker-ce-cli
containerd.io

# Check Docker status
sudo systemctl status docker
```

3.6.3 Testing Your Installation on the Cloud

Run the "Hello, World" test container:

```
bash

docker run hello-world
```

If successful, you'll see Docker pull the image from Docker Hub and print a welcome message. At this point, you can:

- Pull additional images (e.g., `docker run -p 80:80 nginx`).
- Deploy your own containerized apps.
- Integrate this VM into a larger container orchestration setup (e.g., Docker Swarm or Kubernetes).

Conclusion

Installing Docker is the first major step towards modernizing how you build, ship, and run software. Whether you're on Windows, macOS, Linux, or a fresh cloud VM, the process is straightforward—once you understand a few OS-specific nuances and the requirement for virtualization support.

You've also run a "Hello, World" container to validate your setup and gained tips for troubleshooting. Armed with this knowledge, you're ready to dive deeper into Docker's commands, settings, and workflows. From here on out, you'll be able to spin up containers with confidence, transforming how you develop and deploy applications.

In the next chapter, **Chapter 4: Essential Docker Terminology (Jargon-Free)**, we'll break down key Docker terms even further, ensuring you fully understand each building block. We'll also continue providing real-world scenarios so you can see Docker in action.

Key Takeaways

1. **Docker Desktop** Simplifies Installation on **Windows** and **macOS**.
2. **Linux** Users Often Install Docker Engine Directly from Official Repositories.
3. **Verification**: Running `docker run hello-world` Confirms a Successful Setup.
4. **Troubleshooting** Common Issues Often Revolves Around **Virtualization**, **Permissions**, and **Networking**.
5. **Cloud Deployments**: Installing Docker on a Fresh VM (e.g., AWS EC2) Is a Common, Straightforward Practice for Production and Test Environments.

CHAPTER 4

Essential Docker Terminology (Jargon-Free)

Introduction

Having installed Docker in the previous chapter, you're now familiar with running a simple "Hello, World" container. However, Docker has a unique set of terms that can sometimes feel intimidating or confusing to beginners. Terms like **Docker daemon**, **Docker CLI**, **Docker Hub**, **images**, **containers**, and sub-commands such as **run**, **build**, **push**, and **pull** can be overwhelming if presented without context.

In this chapter, we'll break down these terms in a straightforward manner, avoiding heavy technical jargon and focusing on what you actually need to know in day-to-day container work. By the end, you'll have a clear understanding of these concepts and be fully equipped to navigate Docker's ecosystem with confidence.

4.1 Docker Daemon, Docker CLI, and Docker Hub

4.1.1 Docker Daemon: The "Engine Room"

- **What   It   Is**:
  The **Docker daemon** is a background service that runs on your system. Think of it as the "engine room"

of Docker—the part responsible for actually doing the work of building images, running containers, and managing all the resources involved.

- **Why It Matters**: When you tell Docker to run a container or build an image (typically using commands in your terminal), these requests go to the daemon. The daemon then carries out the tasks behind the scenes. You don't usually interact with the daemon directly; instead, you interact with it via the Docker **CLI** (Command-Line Interface) or other tools that talk to Docker.

- **Real-World Analogy**: Imagine a busy restaurant kitchen. You, as the customer, place your order at the front counter. The daemon is like the kitchen staff cooking up your meal—quietly working behind the scenes, turning ingredients into a finished dish. You rarely see the kitchen staff directly, but they're essential for getting your meal ready.

4.1.2 Docker CLI: Your "Control Panel"

- **What It Is**: The **Docker CLI** is the tool you use in your terminal or command prompt to "talk" to the Docker daemon. Commands such as `docker run`, `docker build`, and `docker pull` are all initiated from this CLI. You type your command, the CLI sends your request to the daemon, and then the daemon does the heavy lifting.

- **Why It Matters**: The CLI is how you do most of your day-to-day Docker tasks. Whether you're starting a container, stopping one, or inspecting its logs, you'll typically be using the CLI.

- **Real-World** **Analogy**: Sticking to the restaurant analogy, the CLI is like the cashier or waitstaff at the counter—when you say, "I want a cheeseburger," they relay the request to the kitchen. You interact with the CLI, but it's the daemon (kitchen) that actually makes it happen.

4.1.3 Docker Hub: The "Online Marketplace"

- **What** **It** **Is**: **Docker Hub** is a publicly accessible online registry where people can **publish** and **retrieve** Docker images. It's the default place Docker looks when you run commands like `docker pull nginx` (to download the Nginx image).
- **Why** **It** **Matters**: Docker Hub contains **official images** (maintained by Docker or third-party vendors) and **community images** (created by users around the world). This repository is critical because it's the quickest way to get pre-built images for popular technologies (web servers, databases, programming languages, etc.).
- **Real-World** **Analogy**: If the daemon is your kitchen and the CLI is the cashier, Docker Hub is like a supermarket. You can go there to buy ready-made ingredients (like containers prepackaged with Python, Node.js, or Redis) instead of cooking everything from scratch.

4.2 Images vs. Containers: Understanding the Difference

4.2.1 What Is a Docker Image?

71

- **Definition**:
  A **Docker image** is essentially a blueprint—a collection of files and settings that describe how to run a certain piece of software. It includes everything needed for that software to run: libraries, dependencies, configuration files, and the software itself.
- **Immutable and Layered**:
  When you create a Docker image, it's *read-only*; you can't modify it in place. If you need a new version, you build a new image. Docker also uses a **layered** approach, where each change (like installing a package or copying files) becomes a new layer. If two images share the same layer, Docker only stores that layer once, saving disk space.
- **Real-World Analogy**:
  Think of an image like a **master recipe**. It tells the chef exactly what ingredients and cooking steps are needed to produce a dish. The recipe itself is static— it doesn't change once it's written. If you want a variation (e.g., add extra spices), you create a new recipe version.

4.2.2 What Is a Container?

- **Definition**:
  A **container** is a running instance of an image—like actually cooking that recipe. The container is alive, has processes running, uses memory, and can interact with the network. It's the practical, operational version of the image.
- **Isolation**:
  Each container has its own isolated environment. Even though multiple containers can run on the same machine, they don't step on each other's toes— unless you explicitly allow them to interact.

72

- **Ephemeral   Nature**:
  When a container stops, changes within it aren't
  saved to the original image (unless you specifically
  configure persistent storage). Containers are meant
  to be easy to start and stop—ideal for modern
  DevOps workflows where you frequently update or
  redeploy services.

- **Real-World   Analogy**:
  Continuing the cooking theme: a **container** is the
  actual dish prepared and served. The blueprint
  (image) never changes, but each time you run (cook)
  it, you get a fresh plate of food (container). If you
  throw away the dish, you don't lose the recipe—you
  can always cook another one based on the same
  instructions.

4.3 Key Docker Sub-Commands (Jargon-Free Overview)

Docker provides a variety of sub-commands for different
tasks. Let's focus on the most common ones: **run**, **build**,
push, and **pull**.

4.3.1 `docker run`

- **Purpose**: Start a container from an existing image.
- **Common Usage**:

  bash

  ```
  docker run [OPTIONS] IMAGE [COMMAND]
  ```

  o **Example**:

    bash

```
docker run -d -p 80:80 nginx
```

This command runs a container in the background (-d) using the **nginx** image. It maps port 80 on the container to port 80 on the host, allowing you to access the Nginx server in your browser.

- **What's Actually Happening?**

1. Docker checks if the **nginx** image exists locally. If not, it pulls it from Docker Hub.
    2. Docker creates a new container based on that image.
    3. Docker allocates necessary resources (CPU, memory) and sets up a virtual network for the container.
    4. The container starts running, and you can access it at `http://localhost` on port 80 (in this example).

4.3.2 `docker build`

- **Purpose**: Create a new Docker image from a set of instructions in a **Dockerfile**.
- **Common Usage**:

```bash

docker build [OPTIONS] PATH | URL
```

- o **Example**:

```bash

docker build -t myapp:1.0 .
```

This command looks in the current directory (.)
for a Dockerfile, then builds a new image named
myapp with a tag **1.0**.

- **What's Actually Happening?**

1. Docker reads the **Dockerfile** line by line (e.g., `FROM alpine`, `RUN apt-get install`, `COPY . /app`).
   2. Each instruction creates a new **layer**.
   3. When finished, Docker bundles all layers into a final **image**.
   4. The newly built image is available locally, ready for you to run or push to a registry.

4.3.3 `docker push`

- **Purpose**: Upload a local Docker image to a registry such as Docker Hub (or a private registry).
- **Common Usage**:

```bash
docker push [OPTIONS] NAME[:TAG]
```

  o **Example**:

```bash
docker push myusername/myapp:1.0
```

This command pushes the `myapp:1.0` image to
the Docker Hub account named `myusername`.

- **What's Actually Happening?**

1. Docker looks for the image **myusername/myapp:1.0** in your local image list.
   2. Docker logs in to Docker Hub (if you're not already logged in, it'll prompt you).

75

3. Docker uploads each layer that doesn't already exist on Docker Hub.
4. Once completed, anyone with permission can pull and run **myusername/myapp:1.0** from Docker Hub.

4.3.4 `docker pull`

- **Purpose**: Download an image from a registry (Docker Hub by default) to your local machine.
- **Common Usage**:

```bash

docker pull [OPTIONS] NAME[:TAG]
```

  o **Example**:

```bash

docker pull redis:latest
```

This command downloads the latest version of **redis** from Docker Hub to your local system.

- **What's Actually Happening?**
1. Docker contacts Docker Hub to see if you have permission to pull the image.
2. Docker downloads each layer of the **redis** image.
3. Once finished, you can run a container from it anytime using `docker run`.

4.4 Real-World Example: Pulling and Running a Popular Image (Nginx)

Let's put this terminology into practice with a hands-on example. Suppose you want to run a simple web server using **Nginx**, a popular high-performance HTTP server.

4.4.1 Step 1: Pull the Nginx Image

Open your terminal and type:

```bash
docker pull nginx:latest
```

- **What You're Doing**: You're asking Docker to download the **latest** version of the `nginx` image from Docker Hub.
- **Why It's Useful**: By explicitly pulling the image first, you ensure you have the latest version before running the container.

4.4.2 Step 2: Verify the Download

Check if the image is now on your system:

```bash
docker images
```

You should see something like:

REPOSITORY	TAG	IMAGE ID	CREATED	SIZE
nginx	latest	7e4d58f0e5f3	X weeks ago	133MB

77

The details (IMAGE ID, CREATED date, SIZE) may differ, but **nginx** with tag **latest** should be listed.

4.4.3 Step 3: Run Nginx as a Container

Now, let's start a container:

```bash
docker run -d --name mynginx -p 8080:80 nginx:latest
```

- **Breaking It Down**:
  - o **-d**: Runs the container in "detached" mode (in the background).
  - o **--name mynginx**: Gives the container a friendly name (**mynginx**) so you can refer to it easily later.
  - o **-p 8080:80**: Maps port **80** inside the container to port **8080** on your local machine. Essentially, when you go to `http://localhost:8080`, you're hitting Nginx running in the container.
  - o **nginx:latest**: Tells Docker which image to use.

4.4.4 Step 4: Access the Running Container

- **Open Your Browser**: Go to `http://localhost:8080`. You should see the default **Welcome to nginx!** page.
- **What's Happening Internally**: The container is running the Nginx server on its own internal port **80**, and Docker is forwarding that traffic through your host's port **8080**.

4.4.5 Step 5: Stop or Remove the Container

- **Stop the Container**:

```bash
bash
```

```
docker stop mynginx
```

This gracefully stops Nginx.

- **Remove the Container**:

```bash
bash
```

```
docker rm mynginx
```

Deletes the container instance. The image remains on your system in case you want to re-run it.

That's it! You have successfully pulled and run a popular image from Docker Hub, applying all the key terms—daemon, CLI, image, container, pull, and run—in a single workflow.

4.5 Common Questions About Docker Terminology

1. **Do I Always Need to `pull` an Image Before Running It?**
   - o Not necessarily. When you run docker run, if the image isn't available locally, Docker automatically tries to pull it from Docker Hub (or another registry you specify).
2. **What's the Difference Between `latest` and a Version Tag?**
   - o `latest` usually refers to the newest version of an image, but it can be ambiguous because not all maintainers keep it updated in the same way. A version tag (e.g., nginx:1.21.6) is more explicit. Whenever possible, pin your images to specific versions for consistency.

3. **Can I Modify a Running Container and Save the Changes as a New Image?**
   - Yes, you can commit changes using `docker commit`, but this is generally not best practice in production. It's better to update your **Dockerfile** and rebuild the image for a more controlled, reproducible process.

4. **How Do I Know If Docker Hub Is Safe?**
   - Docker Hub hosts both **official** images (marked with a verified badge) and community images. Always be cautious when pulling community-contributed images. Check official repositories for your needs, or build images yourself if security is a concern.

5. **Is Docker the Only Container Registry?**
   - No. Docker Hub is the most popular, but other registries exist: GitHub Container Registry, Google Container Registry (GCR), Amazon Elastic Container Registry (ECR), and others. The commands `docker pull` and `docker push` still work, but you'd provide a different registry URL (e.g., `us.gcr.io/my-project/my-image:1.0`).

Conclusion

In this chapter, we took a deep dive into Docker's essential terminology—keeping things as jargon-free as possible. We introduced the **Docker daemon** as the behind-the-scenes worker, the **Docker CLI** as your control panel, and **Docker Hub** as the online marketplace for container images. We then clarified the difference between **images** (the read-only blueprint) and **containers** (the live instances you actually run). Finally, we examined core Docker commands—**run, build, push**, and **pull**—demonstrating how each one is used in practice.

By walking through a real-world example of pulling and running **Nginx** from Docker Hub, you've now seen how these concepts come together in a typical workflow. This knowledge will form a solid foundation as you move forward into more advanced topics like **Dockerfiles**, **networking**, **volumes**, and beyond.

In the next chapter, **Chapter 5: First Steps in Docker**, we'll guide you through building, running, and managing your very first containerized application from scratch. We'll also dive into practical tips for daily Docker usage, helping you become more efficient in your container journey.

Key Takeaways

1. **Docker Daemon**: The background service that does the heavy lifting.
2. **Docker CLI**: Your command-line interface for talking to the daemon.
3. **Docker Hub**: A public registry for sharing and downloading images.
4. **Image vs. Container**: An image is a read-only blueprint; a container is the running instance of that image.
5. **Core Commands**:
    o **docker run**: Start a container from an image.
    o **docker build**: Create a new image from a Dockerfile.
    o **docker push**: Upload an image to a registry.
    o **docker pull**: Download an image from a registry.
6. **Practical Example**: Pulling and running **Nginx** demonstrates how these terms and commands fit together in a typical Docker workflow.

CHAPTER 5

First Steps in Docker

Introduction

Up to now, we've explored Docker's core terminology and how to set up your Docker environment. In this chapter, we take a hands-on approach and guide you through creating your first Dockerized application. We'll start by showing you how to write a **Dockerfile**, which defines how to build your application's image. Next, we'll cover key Docker commands—like building and tagging images—and then we'll learn how to start, stop, and inspect running containers.

To make it more concrete, we'll walk through an example Flask-based web application in Python. By the end of this chapter, you'll have a small but functional web app running inside a container, and you'll understand how to manage it either on your local machine or a simple cloud server.

5.1 Why Containerize Your First App?

Moving beyond "Hello, World" examples, containerizing a real application is the best way to understand Docker's power. Docker enables you to:

- **Package** your application along with its dependencies, ensuring it runs the same way everywhere.

- **Simplify Deployment**: Spin up your app with one or two commands, whether you're on a local laptop or a production server.
- **Isolate Environments**: Keep your system clean by running each project in its own container, free from conflicting library versions or outdated packages.

With that in mind, let's roll up our sleeves and dive in.

5.2 Creating a Simple Dockerfile

A **Dockerfile** is a text file that contains instructions Docker uses to build an image. You'll list the base image you're starting from (like Python), copy your application files, and specify how to run your app.

5.2.1 Basic Dockerfile Structure

Here's the general structure you'll commonly see:

```
dockerfile

# (1) Base image
FROM python:3.10-slim

# (2) Set a working directory
WORKDIR /app

# (3) Copy application files
COPY requirements.txt .
COPY . .

# (4) Install dependencies
RUN    pip    install    --no-cache-dir    -r
requirements.txt

# (5) Expose a port
```

```
EXPOSE 5000

# (6) Define the command to run
CMD ["python", "app.py"]
```

Let's break down these instructions:

1. **FROM python:3.10-slim**
   o Declares the base image. Python provides multiple variants, including `slim` (a minimal image) for smaller footprints.
2. **WORKDIR /app**
   o Sets the working directory inside the container. All subsequent commands in the Dockerfile (and your container's runtime environment) will use `/app`.
3. **COPY requirements.txt .** and **COPY . .**
   o Copies files from your local machine into the container image. First, we copy `requirements.txt`, then copy everything else in the current folder (`.`) to `/app` in the container.
4. **RUN pip install --no-cache-dir -r requirements.txt**
   o Installs the Python packages specified in `requirements.txt`. The `--no-cache-dir` flag prevents pip from saving download caches, helping keep the final image size smaller.
5. **EXPOSE 5000**
   o Informs Docker that the container will listen on port 5000 at runtime. This doesn't automatically open the port, but it's useful documentation for anyone running your image.
6. **CMD ["python", "app.py"]**
   o Specifies the command to execute when the container starts. In this case, we're telling Python to run the `app.py` file.

5.2.2 Best Practices

- **Minimize Layers**: Each instruction in a Dockerfile creates a layer. Combine related steps where possible (e.g., copying files together before installing).
- **Leverage .dockerignore**: Similar to `.gitignore`, a `.dockerignore` file tells Docker which files to exclude when building your image (e.g., `.git` folders, large unneeded files).
- **Use Official Images**: Whenever available, start from an official, well-maintained base image (like `python`, `node`, `openjdk`, etc.).

5.3 Building and Tagging Images

Once your Dockerfile is ready, the next step is to build an image. This image becomes the "blueprint" from which containers are launched.

5.3.1 The `docker build` Command

In your terminal, navigate to the folder containing your Dockerfile and application files. Then run:

```bash
docker build -t my-flask-app:1.0 .
```

- **-t my-flask-app:1.0**:
    - o `-t` stands for "tag." You're naming (and optionally versioning) the image.
    - o `my-flask-app` is the repository name, and `1.0` is the tag.
- . at the end indicates the build context is the current directory (where your Dockerfile lives).

As Docker processes each step in your Dockerfile, it will display messages like "Step 1/6" and show the output for each command. Once complete, you can verify success by listing your local images:

```bash
```

```
docker images
```

You should see something like:

REPOSITORY	TAG	IMAGE ID	CREATED	SIZE
my-flask-app	1.0	9a3b1f7xxxxx	About a minute ago	200MB
...	...	...	...	...

5.3.2 Versioning with Tags

Docker images can have multiple tags. For example, you could tag the same image as my-flask-app:latest or my-flask-app:dev. This approach allows you to maintain different stages of your application (development, testing, production) without overwriting each other.

- **Example**:

  ```bash
  ```

  ```
  docker build -t my-flask-app:dev .
  ```

  This new build would be tagged as **my-flask-app:dev** instead of **1.0**.

5.4 Starting, Stopping, and Inspecting Containers

After you've built your image, you're ready to **run** it as a container. Docker's command-line interface (CLI) makes this process simple.

5.4.1 The `docker run` Command

```bash
docker run -d -p 5000:5000 --name flask-container
my-flask-app:1.0
```

Breaking it down:

- **-d**: Runs the container in "detached" mode, so it won't tie up your terminal.
- **-p 5000:5000**: Maps port **5000** inside the container to port **5000** on your local machine. If your Flask app listens on port 5000 (as specified in your code), you'll access it via `http://localhost:5000`.
- **--name flask-container**: Assigns a readable name to your container so you can reference it easily.
- **my-flask-app:1.0**: Specifies the image and tag you're running.

Once you execute this command, Docker starts a new container. You can confirm it's running by checking `docker ps`:

```bash
docker ps
```

You should see a row indicating your container is "Up" and listing the ports it's bound to.

5.4.2 Stopping and Removing Containers

- **Stop a Running Container**:

  bash

  ```
  docker stop flask-container
  ```

  This sends a signal that allows your Flask app to shut down gracefully.

- **Remove (Delete) a Container**:

  bash

  ```
  docker rm flask-container
  ```

  You can only remove a container once it's stopped. Containers are ephemeral, so removing them doesn't affect the image; you can still create another container from the same image at any time.

5.4.3 Inspecting Containers

Sometimes you'll want to see detailed information about a running or stopped container, such as its environment variables, network settings, or the command that started it:

bash

```
docker inspect flask-container
```

This outputs a detailed JSON structure with all the container's configuration data. For quicker lookups:

- **Check Running State**:

```bash
bash

docker ps
```

- **View Real-Time Logs**:

```bash
bash

docker logs flask-container
```

Helpful for troubleshooting errors or seeing incoming requests to your Flask app.

5.5 Real-World Example: Dockerizing a Python/Flask App

Now, let's bring all these steps together in a concrete example. We'll create a minimal Flask application that returns a "Hello, Docker!" message, build it into an image, and run it.

5.5.1 Project Structure

Create a folder called `my-docker-flask-app` with the following files:

```perl
perl

my-docker-flask-app/
 ├─ app.py
 ├─ requirements.txt
 └─ Dockerfile
```

5.5.2 Writing the Flask Application

app.py:

```python
from flask import Flask

app = Flask(__name__)

@app.route('/')
def hello():
    return "Hello, Docker!"

if __name__ == '__main__':
    app.run(host='0.0.0.0', port=5000)
```

Key Points:

- **from flask import Flask**: Imports the Flask framework.
- **app.run(host='0.0.0.0', port=5000)**: Ensures Flask listens on all network interfaces at port **5000**, allowing Docker to map it properly.

5.5.3 Specifying Dependencies

requirements.txt:

```ini
Flask==2.2.2
```

This file tells `pip` which Python packages to install (in this case, just Flask with a specific version).

5.5.4 Creating the Dockerfile

Dockerfile:

```
dockerfile

FROM python:3.10-slim

WORKDIR /app

COPY requirements.txt .
RUN    pip    install    --no-cache-dir    -r
requirements.txt

COPY . .

EXPOSE 5000

CMD ["python", "app.py"]
```

5.5.5 Building the Image

Open a terminal in the **my-docker-flask-app** folder and run:

```bash
bash

docker build -t my-flask-app:1.0 .
```

Docker processes each instruction and assembles the image. After a few seconds or minutes (depending on your internet speed and system resources), you'll have **my-flask-app:1.0** ready.

5.5.6 Running the Container Locally

```bash
bash

docker run -d -p 5000:5000 --name flask-container
my-flask-app:1.0
```

Now open your browser to **http://localhost:5000**. You should see the message:

91

```
Hello, Docker!
```

Check the logs if you'd like:

```
bash

docker logs flask-container
```

You'll see Flask's startup messages and any incoming requests. When you're done:

```
bash

docker stop flask-container
docker rm flask-container
```

5.5.7 Running the Container on a Small Cloud Instance

Assume you have a cloud VM or server (e.g., an AWS EC2 instance or a DigitalOcean droplet) running Ubuntu. You'd follow these steps:

1. **SSH into the Server**:

   ```
   bash

   ssh -i "your-key.pem" ubuntu@your-server-ip
   ```

2. **Install Docker** (if not installed):

   ```
   bash

   sudo apt-get update
   sudo apt-get install docker.io
   sudo systemctl enable docker
   sudo systemctl start docker
   ```

3. **Transfer Your Docker-Files**:
   o You could either push your Docker image to a registry (e.g., Docker Hub) and pull it on the server, or
   o Use **scp** or a Git repository to transfer your Dockerfile and app files, then build it on the server.

Option A: Pull from a Registry

   o First, on your local machine, tag and push the image:

```bash
docker tag my-flask-app:1.0 your-dockerhub-username/my-flask-app:1.0
docker push your-dockerhub-username/my-flask-app:1.0
```

   o On the server:

```bash
docker pull your-dockerhub-username/my-flask-app:1.0
docker run -d -p 5000:5000 --name flask-cloud your-dockerhub-username/my-flask-app:1.0
```

Option B: Build Locally on the Server

   o Copy your files (Dockerfile, app.py, requirements.txt) to the server via **scp** or Git:

```bash
scp -r my-docker-flask-app ubuntu@your-server-ip:~
```

93

o   SSH in and build:

```bash
cd my-docker-flask-app
docker build -t my-flask-app:1.0 .
docker run -d -p 5000:5000 --name
flask-cloud my-flask-app:1.0
```

4. **Access the App**:
   o   In your security group or firewall settings, open port 5000.
   o   Navigate to **http://your-server-ip:5000**.
   o   You should see "Hello, Docker!" just like on your local machine.

This straightforward process is the same pattern you'll use for most Dockerized applications—develop locally, package them into images, and deploy anywhere you want.

5.6 Troubleshooting Tips

1. **Port Conflicts**
   o   If port **5000** is already in use on your system, you can map a different host port, e.g., `-p 8080:5000`, and then access the app at `http://localhost:8080`.
2. **Permissions on Linux**
   o   If you get "permission denied" errors, ensure your user is added to the `docker` group:

```bash
sudo usermod -aG docker $USER
```

Then log out and back in.

3. **Flask Not Responding**
   - o Make sure your Flask app is listening on `host='0.0.0.0'` (not `127.0.0.1`). Otherwise, Docker won't route external requests correctly.
4. **Image Too Large**
   - o Consider using a lighter base image like `python:3.10-alpine` to reduce your final image size. You can also look into multi-stage builds if your application grows more complex.

Conclusion

By creating a simple Dockerfile, building an image, and running a container, you've taken crucial first steps in your Docker journey. You've seen how straightforward it is to wrap a Python/Flask application into a self-contained package and run it both locally and on a cloud instance. Along the way, you learned some best practices and troubleshooting tips that will help you navigate Docker's day-to-day operations with greater confidence.

From here, you can begin to refine your Docker workflow—optimizing image size, adding environment variables, or introducing multiple containers for larger, more complex applications. In the next chapter, **Chapter 6: Dockerfiles in Depth**, we'll dive deeper into best practices for writing Dockerfiles. You'll learn how to craft images that are more efficient, secure, and suitable for production environments.

Key Takeaways

1. **Dockerfile**: Defines how to build your application's image, step by step.
2. **Building Images**: Use `docker build -t <image-name>` . to create an image from your Dockerfile.
3. **Running Containers**: Launch a container with `docker run -d -p HOST_PORT:CONTAINER_PORT <image-name>`.
4. **Managing Containers**: Start, stop, remove, and inspect containers using Docker CLI commands like `docker stop`, `docker rm`, and `docker ps`.
5. **Real-World Workflow**: With a Python/Flask example, you can see how simple it is to containerize and deploy an app locally or in the cloud.

PART II

Deep Diving into Docker's Core Components

CHAPTER 6

Dockerfiles in Depth

Introduction

A **Dockerfile** is the blueprint that Docker uses to assemble an image. Mastering Dockerfiles means you can create lean, secure images that make the most of Docker's capabilities. Poorly written Dockerfiles result in bloated images, security risks, and inefficient development workflows. By contrast, well-crafted Dockerfiles lead to faster builds, smaller images, and production-ready containers that are easier to maintain.

In this chapter, we'll walk you through the most common Dockerfile instructions—explaining exactly how they work, how Docker uses them to create layers, and what each means for your final image. We'll also cover best practices for image optimization and crucial security considerations, such as running containers with non-root privileges. Finally, you'll see how to transform a messy, inefficient Dockerfile into a concise, optimized version that's ready for production deployment.

6.1 The Building Blocks: Common Dockerfile Instructions

A Dockerfile is essentially a list of commands and settings. Each instruction creates or modifies layers in your final image. Below are the most commonly used instructions:

6.1.1 FROM

- **Purpose**: Declares the **base image** from which you are building.
- **Example**:

```dockerfile
FROM ubuntu:20.04
```

- **Usage   Tip**:
  Always start with a minimal and official base image unless you have a specific reason to do otherwise. For instance, if you only need Python, `python:3.10-slim` might be more optimal than `ubuntu:20.04`.

6.1.2 RUN

- **Purpose**: Executes a command in a new layer on top of the current image and commits the results.
- **Example**:

```dockerfile
RUN apt-get update && apt-get install -y curl
```

- **Usage   Tip**:
  Combine multiple commands into one RUN instruction when appropriate. This reduces the number of image layers. However, be mindful that overly long RUN commands can become unwieldy.

6.1.3 COPY and ADD

- **Purpose**: Copy files from your host (the build context) into the container's filesystem.
- **Example**:

```
dockerfile

COPY app.py /usr/src/app/
```

- **Usage Tip**:
  - o **COPY** is generally preferred for straightforward file copies.
  - o **ADD** can automatically unpack compressed files or pull files from URLs, but this can make builds less transparent. Use ADD sparingly or only when its extra functionality is needed.

6.1.4 WORKDIR

- **Purpose**: Sets the **working directory** for subsequent instructions.
- **Example**:

```
dockerfile

WORKDIR /usr/src/app
```

- **Usage**   **Tip**:
  Simplifies commands like RUN and COPY because you don't have to specify absolute paths over and over.

6.1.5 ENV

- **Purpose**: Sets environment variables that persist through the build and container runtime.
- **Example**:

```
dockerfile

ENV APP_ENV=production
```

- **Usage**   **Tip**:
  Use this to define configuration values (e.g., API URLs,

app environment). Be cautious about storing sensitive data like passwords or tokens directly in an ENV instruction.

6.1.6 EXPOSE

- **Purpose**: Documents the port(s) your container will listen on at runtime.
- **Example**:

```dockerfile
EXPOSE 8080
```

- **Usage**   **Tip**:
This doesn't automatically publish the port. You still need to use the -p flag when running the container. However, **EXPOSE** helps other developers understand which ports your app expects to receive traffic on.

6.1.7 CMD vs. ENTRYPOINT

- **Purpose**: Define how the container starts—what command or script it should run by default.
- **Example (CMD)**:

```dockerfile
CMD ["node", "app.js"]
```

- **Example (ENTRYPOINT)**:

```dockerfile
ENTRYPOINT ["python"]
CMD ["app.py"]
```

- **Usage Tip**:

101

- o **ENTRYPOINT** defines the container's main executable. **CMD** can then provide default arguments.
- o If you need to override the default command frequently, use **CMD**. If your container's main purpose is to run one process, use **ENTRYPOINT**.
- o Combining them allows for flexible customization (e.g., specifying command-line arguments at runtime).

6.1.8 HEALTHCHECK

- **Purpose**: Instructs Docker how to test the container to confirm that it's working correctly.
- **Example**:

```dockerfile
HEALTHCHECK  --interval=30s  --timeout=5s
CMD  curl  -f  http://localhost:8080/health
|| exit 1
```

- **Usage   Tip**:
  Useful for production environments where you need containers to report their own health to orchestrators like Kubernetes or Docker Swarm.

6.2 Best Practices for Image Optimization

A well-optimized Dockerfile can dramatically reduce build times and final image sizes. This not only speeds up local development but also lowers bandwidth and storage costs when deploying to servers.

6.2.1 Layering and Caching

Docker builds images in **layers**, caching each step. If a layer hasn't changed, Docker uses the cached version instead of rebuilding it from scratch.

- **Order   Matters**: Put the most frequently changing instructions (like copying your application source code) **near the bottom** of the Dockerfile. Keep the base, dependency, and environment setup **near the top** so they don't get rebuilt needlessly.
- **Cache   Invalidation**: If you modify a line that's high in the Dockerfile, **every subsequent layer** will be rebuilt. This can significantly slow down the build process.

6.2.2 Combining Commands

For instance, instead of:

```dockerfile
RUN apt-get update
RUN apt-get install -y curl
```

Use:

```dockerfile
RUN apt-get update && apt-get install -y curl
```

This approach creates **fewer layers**, saving space and speeding up builds. However, avoid writing excessively long commands that become unreadable—balance readability with layer optimization.

6.2.3 Using Slim or Alpine Base Images

Many official images have **slim** or **alpine** variants:

- **Example**:
  - o   `python:3.10` vs. `python:3.10-slim` vs. `python:3.10-alpine`
  - o   `node:16` vs. `node:16-alpine`

Using these minimal images can reduce your final image size substantially. However, be mindful that **alpine** uses **musl libc** instead of **glibc**, which can cause compatibility issues with certain libraries.

6.3 Minimizing Security Risks

Security is paramount when building production images. Docker provides several guidelines for reducing your attack surface.

6.3.1 Running as Non-Root User

By default, containers often run as **root** inside the container, which can be risky if an attacker breaks out of the application. Instead, create a **non-root user** and switch to it in your Dockerfile:

```dockerfile
RUN groupadd -r appuser && useradd -r -g appuser appuser
USER appuser
```

This way, even if your container is compromised, the attacker won't have root privileges on the host system.

6.3.2 Using Trusted Base Images

104

Always start with **official or trusted** base images. Avoid random, unverified images from public registries. If you need custom functionality, build your own base image from a reputable source.

6.3.3 Regularly Updating Dependencies

Keep an eye on updates to your base image and installed packages. Outdated software can contain known vulnerabilities. Use tools like `apt-get update && apt-get upgrade -y` (in Debian-based distributions) or package-specific security scanners.

6.3.4 Secrets Management

Don't store passwords, API keys, or other secrets in Dockerfiles or environment variables checked into source control. Use Docker's built-in **secrets** (especially on Swarm or Kubernetes) or external secret managers like **HashiCorp Vault** or **AWS Secrets Manager**.

6.4 Real-World Example: Transforming a Large, Unwieldy Dockerfile

Let's consider a scenario: you have a monolithic Node.js application with multiple dependencies, environment variables, and build steps. The original Dockerfile looks something like this:

```dockerfile
FROM node:16

# Application code
```

```
COPY package.json /app/package.json
WORKDIR /app
RUN npm install

COPY . /app

ENV NODE_ENV=production
ENV PORT=3000
ENV API_KEY=supersecretkey

EXPOSE 3000

RUN apt-get update
RUN apt-get install -y curl
RUN rm -rf /var/lib/apt/lists/*

CMD ["npm", "start"]
```

6.4.1 Observations and Issues

1. **Security Risk**: Sensitive API keys are stored in environment variables inside the Dockerfile.
2. **Multiple RUN Instructions**: Each RUN creates a new layer. This is not optimized for layering.
3. **No Non-Root User**: The container runs as root by default.
4. **Redundant apt-get Steps**: We can combine apt-get update and apt-get install in one layer, then clean up in the same step.

6.4.2 Optimized and Secure Dockerfile

Below is a revised version with improvements in layering, security, and user privileges:

```
dockerfile

# 1. Use an official, minimal base image.
FROM node:16-alpine

# 2. Create and switch to a non-root user.
```

106

```
# Alpine uses 'addgroup' and 'adduser' commands
slightly differently than Debian-based distros.
RUN addgroup -g 1001 appgroup \
    && adduser -D -u 1001 -G appgroup appuser

# 3. Set working directory
WORKDIR /app

# 4. Copy package.json and install dependencies
#     This leverages Docker's caching by copying
package.json separately.
COPY package.json package-lock.json /app/
RUN npm install --production

# 5. Copy the rest of the application source
COPY . /app

# 6. Expose the application port
EXPOSE 3000

# 7. Switch to non-root user
USER appuser

# 8. Set environment variables at runtime (avoid
embedding secrets)
# ENV NODE_ENV=production
# ENV API_KEY=supersecretkey (commented out -
we'll pass it at runtime instead)
# We'll pass these via 'docker run -e ...' or in
an orchestration tool.

# 9. Define the default command
CMD ["npm", "start"]
```

What Changed?

1. **Alpine Base**: Switched from `node:16` to `node:16-alpine`, shrinking the image size.
2. **Non-Root User**: Created a user with an ID of `1001`, ensuring the container doesn't run as root.
3. **Layering**:
   o Separate copying of `package.json` and `npm install` from copying the rest of the source

code. This ensures Docker can cache the dependencies layer if `package.json` hasn't changed.

- o Combined certain commands to reduce the number of layers.

4. **Security**:
   - o Moved sensitive environment variables out of the Dockerfile. We'll supply them at runtime with `docker run -e API_KEY="secret"` ... or use a docker-compose file or orchestrator.
   - o By using `USER appuser`, any compromise within the container won't have root access.

5. **Smaller Footprint**: Using Alpine and caching strategies can reduce this image from hundreds of MB to potentially under 100MB, depending on the app's dependencies.

6.4.3 Building and Running the Optimized Dockerfile

```bash
docker build -t my-node-app:optimized .
docker run -d \
  -p 3000:3000 \
  -e NODE_ENV=production \
  -e API_KEY="secret" \
  --name node-app \
  my-node-app:optimized
```

With these changes:

- Your builds run faster because Docker caches layers effectively.
- Your final image is smaller, saving storage space on your local machine and any cloud registry.
- You've removed hardcoded secrets, reducing the risk of exposing sensitive data.
- You're following the principle of least privilege by using a non-root user.

Conclusion

Dockerfiles are at the heart of every Docker image, and understanding how to write them well is critical for creating efficient, secure, and production-ready containers. By mastering the basic instructions—**FROM, RUN, COPY, CMD**, etc.—and following best practices like combining commands, leveraging caching, and avoiding root privileges, you can drastically improve your containerization workflow.

In this chapter, we dissected each core Dockerfile instruction, explored optimization techniques related to layering and caching, and reviewed security measures such as running as a non-root user and managing secrets securely. We then illustrated how to transform a large, unwieldy Dockerfile into a streamlined, production-friendly version.

Next, in **Chapter 7: Docker Images: Creation and Management**, we'll go deeper into how Docker images are structured, how to version and tag images effectively, and how to work with image registries beyond Docker Hub, including private registries. You'll learn more about scanning images for vulnerabilities and best practices for maintaining a clean, organized image repository.

Key Takeaways

1. **Core Dockerfile Instructions**: FROM, RUN, COPY, WORKDIR, EXPOSE, CMD, ENTRYPOINT, ENV, HEALTHCHECK.
2. **Optimizing Image Builds**:

- o Minimize layers by combining commands.
- o Order Dockerfile instructions wisely to leverage caching.
- o Consider using slim or alpine variants of base images.

3. **Security Best Practices**:
   - o Avoid running containers as root.
   - o Keep secrets and sensitive data out of Dockerfiles.
   - o Use trusted base images and regularly update dependencies.

4. **Real-World Transformation**:
   - o Switching to a minimal base image, adopting a non-root user, and removing hardcoded secrets can significantly improve both security and performance.

5. **Production-Ready Dockerfiles**:
   - o Focus on reproducibility, security, and efficiency.
   - o A well-crafted Dockerfile streamlines deployment, reduces costs, and enhances reliability.

CHAPTER 7

Docker Images: Creation and Management

Introduction

In the previous chapter, you learned how to write Dockerfiles in a secure and optimized way. That knowledge is foundational to creating Docker images. But how exactly do Docker images work under the hood? What is the layering concept that helps Docker optimize storage and reduce redundancy? How do you properly tag and version your images so that development, staging, and production environments don't get mixed up? And finally, how do you store and share your images—whether on Docker Hub or within a private registry?

This chapter answers these questions and more, giving you a practical guide to **image creation and management**. By the end, you'll know how to use Docker's layering model effectively, adopt best practices for image tagging, and decide whether to host your images on Docker Hub or in a private registry. You'll also walk through a real-world example of tagging and pushing multiple versions of a microservice to a private repository.

7.1 Understanding Docker's Image Layering Concept

7.1.1 How Layering Works

Every Docker image is built in **layers**. When you run a `docker build` command that processes each instruction in your Dockerfile (e.g., `FROM`, `RUN`, `COPY`), Docker creates a new layer for each instruction. Layers are essentially read-only snapshots that build upon each other to form the final image.

- **Why Layers?**
  - **Efficiency**: If two images share certain layers, Docker will only store those layers once on your machine.
  - **Caching**: When you rebuild an image, Docker reuses unchanged layers from its cache, speeding up build times.

7.1.2 Example of Layering

Consider this simplified Dockerfile:

```dockerfile
FROM python:3.10-slim
WORKDIR /app
COPY requirements.txt .
RUN pip install --no-cache-dir -r requirements.txt
COPY . .
CMD ["python", "app.py"]
```

- **Layer 1**: Base image (`FROM python:3.10-slim`)
- **Layer 2**: `WORKDIR /app`
- **Layer 3**: Copy `requirements.txt`
- **Layer 4**: Install dependencies (`RUN pip install...`)
- **Layer 5**: Copy the rest of the files (`COPY . .`)
- **Layer 6**: Final layer specifying the default command (`CMD ["python", "app.py"]`)

112

If you update `app.py` but don't touch `requirements.txt`, Docker won't rebuild layers 1 to 4 on subsequent builds, saving time and resources.

7.2 Tagging and Versioning Strategies

7.2.1 The Role of Tags

A **tag** is a label attached to an image that helps you identify its version or purpose. When you run `docker build -t myapp:1.0 .`, you're naming the image **myapp** and tagging it with **1.0**. If you don't specify a tag, Docker defaults to **latest**, but that tag can often be misleading if not managed carefully.

7.2.2 Common Tagging Conventions

1. **Semantic Versioning**:
   - `myapp:1.0`, `myapp:1.1`, `myapp:2.0`, etc.
   - Aligns with your application's release versions, helping teams track which image corresponds to which release.
2. **Release Channels**:
   - `myapp:dev`, `myapp:staging`, `myapp:prod`
   - Indicates the environment or "channel" the image is intended for. For instance, you might build a `dev` image for testing, then create a `prod` image from the tested version.
3. **Git Commit Tags**:
   - `myapp:abcdef1`
   - Tagging the image with a short commit hash ensures a direct link between your image and the exact commit that built it. This is popular in CI/CD pipelines.

113

7.2.3 Best Practices for Tagging

- **Avoid Overusing `latest`**: It can be convenient, but it's risky if multiple versions of your app end up sharing the same tag.
- **Pin Dependencies**: If your image relies on a specific version of a language or base image, reflect that in your tag. For example, `python:3.10-slim` vs. just `python:3-slim`.
- **Automate in CI/CD**: Have your pipeline tag images with both a semantic version and a commit hash. That way, you get both readability and traceability.

7.3 Storing and Sharing Images: Docker Hub vs. Private Registries

7.3.1 Docker Hub

Docker Hub is the default public registry Docker uses. When you type `docker pull nginx`, Docker looks at Docker Hub and fetches the **nginx** image if you haven't already got it locally.

Pros:

- Huge community and official images.
- Easy to get started.
- Basic features like automated builds and webhooks.

Cons:

- Public by default (unless you pay for private repos, which have limited free private repositories for personal accounts).

- Might not comply with strict data sovereignty rules in some organizations.

7.3.2 Private Registries

Private registries let you store and share images within your organization, without exposing them to the public internet. Options include:

1. **Docker Registry (Open Source)**: The official open-source registry you can host on your own servers.
2. **GitHub Container Registry**: Tightly integrated with GitHub repositories.
3. **Cloud-Specific**: AWS Elastic Container Registry (ECR), Google Container Registry (GCR), and Azure Container Registry (ACR).
4. **Other Third-Party Solutions**: JFrog Artifactory, Harbor, etc.

Pros:

- Full control over access and security.
- Can integrate with your existing infrastructure (CI/CD pipelines, user accounts, etc.).
- Often meets compliance or data governance requirements.

Cons:

- Requires setup and maintenance.
- May introduce extra steps for user authentication if you're not integrating with a cloud provider's services.

7.3.3 Deciding Which Registry to Use

- **Small Projects or Personal Use**: Docker Hub is great if you don't need strict privacy or compliance.

- **Enterprise or Regulated Industries**: A private registry is usually mandatory to keep your images and intellectual property secure.
- **Hybrid Approach**: Use Docker Hub for open-source or public images, and maintain a private registry for proprietary applications.

7.4 Real-World Example: Tagging and Pushing a Microservice to a Private Registry

Imagine you have a microservice named **payment-service**. You want to maintain different versions—like **v1.0, v1.1**, and **latest**—and store them in a private registry to keep your proprietary code secure.

7.4.1 Step 1: Build Your Docker Image

Assuming you have a Dockerfile in the **payment-service** folder:

```bash
cd payment-service
docker build -t payment-service:1.0 .
```

This command creates an image named `payment-service` with the tag `1.0`.

7.4.2 Step 2: Tag the Image for Your Private Registry

Let's say your private registry is at `registry.mycompany.com`. You tag the image to indicate its location:

```
bash
```

```
docker          tag          payment-service:1.0
registry.mycompany.com/payment-service:1.0
```

If you also want a **latest** tag:

```
bash
```

```
docker          tag          payment-service:1.0
registry.mycompany.com/payment-service:latest
```

Now you have two tags pointing to the same image, but set up for your private registry.

7.4.3 Step 3: Authenticate to Your Private Registry

If your registry requires authentication, log in via Docker CLI:

```
bash
```

```
docker login registry.mycompany.com
```

You'll be prompted for your username and password (or a token, depending on your setup).

7.4.4 Step 4: Push Your Image

```
bash
```

```
docker    push    registry.mycompany.com/payment-
service:1.0
docker    push    registry.mycompany.com/payment-
service:latest
```

Docker will upload each layer that isn't already in your private registry. Once complete, anyone with credentials to

registry.mycompany.com can pull **payment-service:1.0** or **payment-service:latest**.

7.4.5 Step 5: Verify and Pull the Image

On any other machine with Docker, you can log in and pull your microservice:

bash

```
docker login registry.mycompany.com
docker pull registry.mycompany.com/payment-service:1.0
```

After pulling the image, you can run it:

bash

```
docker run -d --name payment-service -p 8080:8080
registry.mycompany.com/payment-service:1.0
```

7.4.6 Updating to a New Version

When you release a new version (say **v1.1**):

1. Build and tag it:

    bash

    ```
    docker build -t payment-service:1.1 .
    docker tag payment-service:1.1
    registry.mycompany.com/payment-service:1.1
    ```

2. Push it to the registry:

    bash

```
docker                          push
registry.mycompany.com/payment-
service:1.1
```

3. Optionally update `latest`:

```
bash
```

```
docker        tag        payment-service:1.1
registry.mycompany.com/payment-
service:latest
docker                          push
registry.mycompany.com/payment-
service:latest
```

This workflow ensures older versions remain accessible (like **v1.0**), while **latest** points to your newest stable release (v1.1).

Conclusion

Docker images are the lifeblood of containerized applications, and understanding how to manage them effectively is a cornerstone of modern DevOps. By grasping the layering concept, you can optimize builds and store images efficiently. Through thoughtful tagging and versioning strategies, you'll maintain clear boundaries between development, staging, and production environments, reducing the likelihood of versioning mix-ups. And by selecting the right registry—whether Docker Hub, a private service, or a hybrid approach—you'll balance ease of access with security and compliance.

In this chapter, you saw how Docker uses **layers** to avoid redundant storage, why **tagging** is crucial for organizing and versioning images, and how to **push** your images to both

Docker Hub and private registries. The real-world example of tagging and pushing a microservice demonstrated a common workflow you'll likely adopt in your own projects.

Next up, in **Chapter 8: Docker Containers: Lifecycle and Best Practices**, we'll shift our focus from images to the lifecycle of containers—how they're created, started, stopped, paused, and removed. You'll also learn best practices for managing containers at scale, including ways to handle persistent data, logs, and more.

Key Takeaways

1. **Docker Images Use Layering**: Each instruction in a Dockerfile creates a layer, allowing for caching and storage efficiency.
2. **Tagging & Versioning**: Essential for distinguishing various builds, release channels, and application stages. Avoid over-reliance on `latest`.
3. **Registry Options**:
   - **Docker Hub** is the default public registry with vast community support.
   - **Private Registries** (like AWS ECR, GCR, or self-hosted) offer more security and control.
4. **Real-World Example**: Tagging and pushing a microservice (e.g., `v1`, `v1.1`, `latest`) to a private registry is a common, repeatable workflow.
5. **Efficient & Organized**: Proper image management streamlines deployment pipelines and keeps your infrastructure lean and orderly.

CHAPTER 8

Docker Containers: Lifecycle and Best Practices

Introduction

In previous chapters, we focused on how Docker images are created, managed, and shared. Now, let's turn our attention to **containers**—the live, running instances of those images. Understanding how containers move through their lifecycle (from creation to removal) is critical for effectively managing them in real-world scenarios.

In this chapter, we'll break down the various **container states** (create, start, stop, pause, remove), discuss **persistent storage** strategies to retain data beyond a container's lifespan, and compare **background** (detached) mode vs. **interactive** mode. By the end, you'll be equipped with the knowledge to handle containers gracefully, whether you're building a development environment on your local machine or orchestrating services in a production cluster.

8.1 Docker Container Lifecycle

A container's journey typically follows these stages: **create**, **start**, **stop**, **pause**, **unpause**, and **remove**. Understanding each step helps you manage containers efficiently.

8.1.1 Create

- **docker create**
  - o This command sets up the container's filesystem, network settings, and more, but does **not** start the container.
  - o Often, you'll use `docker run` instead of `docker create`, because `docker run` handles both creation and starting in one command.

8.1.2 Start

- **docker start**
  - o This transitions a stopped or newly created container into a running state.
  - o If you used `docker create` initially, you must manually run `docker start <container_name>` or `<container_id>` to begin execution.

8.1.3 Stop

- **docker stop**
  - o Sends a signal (SIGTERM by default) to the main process inside the container, giving it time to shut down gracefully before forcibly killing it.
  - o If your application needs extra time to clean up, you can specify a timeout: `docker stop -t 30 mycontainer`.

8.1.4 Pause / Unpause

- **docker pause / docker unpause**
  - o Freezes all processes in the container, then resumes them.
  - o Useful for brief maintenance windows or debugging scenarios where you need to halt container activity without stopping it entirely.

8.1.5 Remove

- **docker rm**
    - o Permanently deletes the container and frees up associated resources.
    - o If a container is still running, you must stop it first (or use `docker rm -f` to force removal).
    - o **Ephemeral Nature**: Docker containers are often treated as temporary. When one is removed, any data not stored in a volume or bind mount is lost.

8.2 Persistent Storage Strategies

Containers are **ephemeral** by design—once removed, all data inside them disappears. However, many real-world applications need to retain data (e.g., database files, configuration data, or user-uploaded content). Docker provides several options:

8.2.1 Volumes

- **What They Are**:
    - o A **volume** is a dedicated storage area managed by Docker, kept outside the container's filesystem.
    - o Docker volumes live in Docker's internal directory (e.g., `/var/lib/docker/volumes` on Linux).
- **Advantages**:
    - o Data persists even if the container is removed or replaced.
    - o Volumes can be shared across multiple containers.
    - o You can back up or migrate volumes easily.
- **How to Use**:

```bash
```

```
docker run -d \
  -v mydata:/var/lib/mysql \
  --name mydb \
  mysql:latest
```

Here, **mydata** is a named volume storing MySQL data.

8.2.2 Bind Mounts

- **What They Are**:
  - o A **bind mount** links a directory on the host machine to a directory in the container.
  - o Changes in one reflect in the other—handy for local development.
- **Advantages**:
  - o Useful for reading and writing files from the host's filesystem in real time.
  - o Great for local dev environments where you want your code changes to appear instantly in the container.
- **How to Use**:

```bash
docker run -d \
  -v /path/on/host:/path/in/container \
  --name webapp \
  node:latest
```

This setup gives the container direct access to the host's /path/on/host directory.

8.2.3 Temporary vs. Persistent

- **tmpfs Mounts**:

- o Used for sensitive data that shouldn't persist on disk (e.g., ephemeral caches or security tokens).
  - o Data remains in memory—once the container stops, the data is gone.
- **Deciding Which to Use**:
  - o **Volumes** are generally preferred for production due to easier management and portability.
  - o **Bind mounts** make local development simpler, as you can edit files in your IDE and instantly see changes in the container.
  - o **tmpfs** is ideal for short-term data that you don't want written to disk.

8.3 Running Containers: Background vs. Interactive Mode

8.3.1 Detached (Background) Mode

- **docker run -d**
  - o Starts the container and **detaches** it from your current terminal session.
  - o You can continue using your terminal while the container runs in the background.
  - o Standard for servers, microservices, and any application that doesn't need direct user input.
- **Monitoring**:
  - o Use `docker logs <container_name>` to view the container's console output.
  - o Use `docker exec -it <container_name> bash` (or `sh`) to attach an interactive shell for diagnostics or maintenance.

8.3.2 Interactive Mode

- **docker run -it**

125

- o Attaches your terminal to the container's standard input and output.
- o Commonly used for running a one-off task, debugging, or exploring the container environment.
- **Examples**:

```
bash

docker run -it ubuntu:latest bash
```

This spins up a temporary Ubuntu container, dropping you into a shell session.

8.3.3 Choosing the Right Mode

- **Servers / Daemons**: Usually run in **detached** mode.
- **Debugging / One-Off Scripts**: Usually run in **interactive** mode.

8.4 Real-World Example: Managing Multiple Containers in a Dev Environment

Let's say you're developing a microservice-based application with three services:

1. **Auth Service** (Node.js on port 3001)
2. **User Profile Service** (Python/Flask on port 3002)
3. **Web Frontend** (React on port 3000)

You need to run these containers simultaneously for local development.

8.4.1 Directory Structure

```
pgsql

microservices/
├── auth-service/
│   ├── Dockerfile
│   ├── package.json
│   └── index.js
├── user-service/
│   ├── Dockerfile
│   ├── requirements.txt
│   └── app.py
└── web-frontend/
    ├── Dockerfile
    ├── package.json
    └── src/
```

Each service has its own Dockerfile defining how to build that particular service.

8.4.2 Building and Tagging Each Service

```bash
bash

# Auth service
cd auth-service
docker build -t auth-service:dev .

# User Profile service
cd ../user-service
docker build -t user-service:dev .

# Web Frontend
cd ../web-frontend
docker build -t web-frontend:dev .
```

8.4.3 Running in Detached Mode with Shared Network

You want these containers to communicate with each other via a custom Docker network. For instance:

```
bash

docker network create microservices-net
```

Now start each container on that network:

```
bash

# Auth service
docker run -d \
  --network microservices-net \
  -p 3001:3001 \
  --name auth-service-dev \
  auth-service:dev

# User Profile service
docker run -d \
  --network microservices-net \
  -p 3002:3002 \
  --name user-service-dev \
  user-service:dev

# Web Frontend
docker run -d \
  --network microservices-net \
  -p 3000:3000 \
  --name web-frontend-dev \
  web-frontend:dev
```

Key Points:

- **-d** runs each container in the background.
- **--network microservices-net** puts them all on the same virtual network for easy inter-service communication.
- **-p** maps container ports to your host machine so you can access them via localhost:<port>.

8.4.4 Verifying and Inspecting

- **List running containers**:

```bash
docker ps
```

You should see all three services running with their respective ports and names.

- **Logs**:

```bash
docker logs auth-service-dev
docker logs user-service-dev
docker logs web-frontend-dev
```

Check each service's console output for startup messages or errors.

- **Testing**:
  - o Access the **Web Frontend** at `http://localhost:3000`.
  - o The frontend calls the **Auth Service** on `http://auth-service-dev:3001` (internal Docker DNS) or `http://localhost:3001` from your host.
  - o Similarly, it calls the **User Service** at `http://user-service-dev:3002`.
  - o Communication within the Docker network uses container names as hostnames, allowing each service to find the others seamlessly.

8.4.5 Using Volumes (Development Bind Mount)

During development, you might want real-time code edits. You can mount local source code into the container:

```bash
```

```
docker run -d \
  -p 3001:3001 \
  --name auth-service-dev \
  --network microservices-net \
  -v "$(pwd)":/usr/src/app \
  auth-service:dev
```

Now, any changes you make on your local machine inside the **auth-service** folder appear immediately inside the container.

Conclusion

Containers are ephemeral by nature, but their lifecycle—from creation to removal—can be managed in ways that align with real-world application needs. Understanding the distinct container states helps you operate containers smoothly, whether you're pausing them for quick maintenance or shutting them down gracefully. Persistent storage strategies—like volumes and bind mounts—bridge the gap between ephemeral containers and long-lived data. Meanwhile, choosing between detached mode and interactive mode allows you to flexibly handle use cases ranging from production-ready microservices to quick debugging sessions.

In this chapter, we also explored a practical scenario of managing multiple containers in a local development environment. By creating a shared network and running services in separate containers, you can replicate a microservices architecture on your own machine, closely mirroring how you'll deploy the same services to production.

In the next chapter, **Chapter 9: Working with Data and Volumes**, we'll dive deeper into persistent storage, focusing on how to back up, migrate, and secure your volumes for both development and production contexts.

Key Takeaways

1. **Container Lifecycle**:
   - **Create → Start → Stop → Remove**.
   - **Pause/Unpause** for halting container processes without fully stopping the container.
2. **Persistent Storage**:
   - **Volumes** (Docker-managed) vs. **Bind Mounts** (direct host directory).
   - **tmpfs** for in-memory data that shouldn't persist.
3. **Background vs. Interactive Mode**:
   - Use **detached** mode (-d) for services and daemons.
   - Use **interactive** mode (-it) for debugging or one-off tasks.
4. **Real-World Example**: Managing multiple microservices in a local dev environment highlights best practices like Docker networks, port mapping, and using volumes for rapid development.
5. **Ephemeral Containers, Permanent Data**: Docker's ephemeral nature isn't a barrier to storing data—just follow best practices for volumes and bind mounts.

CHAPTER 9

Working with Data and Volumes

Introduction

Docker containers are intentionally **ephemeral**—meaning if you remove a container, any data stored within it disappears unless you make specific provisions to persist it. While this design is ideal for stateless services, many real-world applications need to retain data. For instance, databases, file uploads, logs, and other critical data must survive container restarts and removals.

In this chapter, we'll explore how to store data persistently using **Docker volumes** and **bind mounts**. You'll learn how to back up and migrate volumes, ensuring your data remains safe and portable. We'll also delve into best practices and security considerations, such as encryption and access controls, so that your sensitive information remains secure. By the end, you'll have the knowledge to manage data like a pro—whether you're running a local development stack or a production environment.

9.1 Docker Volumes vs. Bind Mounts

9.1.1 Docker Volumes

Definition:
A **volume** is a special directory on the host filesystem managed by Docker. When you create or run a container that

uses a volume, Docker automatically stores data in a location such as `/var/lib/docker/volumes` (on Linux).

- **Creation**:
  - o **Named volumes**: Created explicitly by name (`docker volume create my_volume`) or implicitly when you use `-v my_volume:/path/in/container`.
  - o **Anonymous volumes**: Docker assigns a random name if you just specify `-v /path/in/container` without a name.
- **Benefits**:
1. **Persistence**: Even if containers are removed, the volume persists until you explicitly remove it.
   2. **Portability**: Volumes can be attached to new containers, making it easier to upgrade or replace containers without losing data.
   3. **Performance**: Typically faster I/O than bind mounts because volumes leverage Docker's storage driver optimizations.
   4. **Security**: Access to volumes is governed by Docker rather than your host's entire filesystem.
- **Use Cases**:
  - o Database storage (MySQL, PostgreSQL)
  - o Persistent application logs or uploaded files
  - o Shared data between multiple containers

9.1.2 Bind Mounts

Definition:
A **bind mount** maps a host directory directly to a directory within the container. Changes in one immediately reflect in the other.

- **Creation**:

```bash
```

133

```
docker run -d \
  -v /host/path:/container/path \
  --name my_container \
  my_image
```

- **Benefits**:
  1. **Direct Access**: You can instantly modify files on your host, and those changes appear in the container (great for local development).
  2. **No Extra Setup**: No need to create or manage a Docker-specific volume—just pick a directory on the host.
- **Drawbacks**:
  1. **Security Risks**: If you map a sensitive host directory, you risk exposing it.
  2. **Platform Specifics**: File path syntax may vary between Linux, macOS, and Windows.
  3. **Less Isolation**: The container can read/write directly to your host's filesystem, which might not be ideal in all scenarios.
- **Use Cases**:
  o Local dev environments (e.g., mounting the source code folder).
  o Sharing configuration files that are already managed by the host.
  o Quick access to logs or data without dealing with Docker volume commands.

9.1.3 Choosing the Right Approach

- **Volumes** are generally better for production services where data needs to persist independently of container lifecycle.
- **Bind mounts** are well-suited for development, debugging, or situations where you explicitly need to share a host directory in real time.

9.2 Backing Up and Migrating Volumes

Data stored in Docker volumes is crucial for many applications—particularly databases. Regular backups and easy migration ensure data safety and portability.

9.2.1 Backup Strategies

1. **Docker CLI**: You can temporarily spin up a container that mounts your volume and runs a backup command.

   ```bash
   bash

   docker run --rm \
     -v my_volume:/data \
     -v $(pwd):/backup \
     ubuntu \
     tar czf /backup/my_volume_backup.tar.gz /data
   ```

   o **Explanation**:
   - **--rm**: Removes the container after it finishes running.
   - **-v my_volume:/data**: Mounts the volume at /data.
   - **-v $(pwd):/backup**: Mounts your current host directory as /backup to store the resulting tar file.
   - **ubuntu**: Using a base Ubuntu image.
   - **tar czf /backup/my_volume_backup.tar. gz /data**: Archives the data from /data (the volume) into my_volume_backup.tar.gz in the /backup directory (on the host).

2. **Application-Level Backup**: Use your database's own backup tools (e.g., PostgreSQL pg_dump) or

135

application-specific backup scripts. This often provides more consistent backups, especially if the app needs to be paused or locked.

3. **Scheduled Jobs**: Automate backups using cron jobs, CI/CD pipelines, or orchestration platforms (like Kubernetes CronJobs). Store the backups in remote storage (S3, GCS, etc.) for disaster recovery.

9.2.2 Migrating Volumes

- **Same Host Migration**:
  - o If you're moving from one container to another on the same host, you can simply point the new container to the same named volume.
- **New Host Migration**:
  - o Export your volume using the tar approach above, then copy the archive to the new host.
  - o Create a new volume on the target host, and extract the archive into it with a similar tar command.

Pro Tip: For large volumes, consider using **rsync** or tools that support incremental transfers to speed up the migration process.

9.3 Security Considerations for Storing Sensitive Data

9.3.1 Least Privilege

- **Non-Root Containers**: Run containers as non-root users to reduce the risk of malicious access to host data.
- **Permissions and Ownership**: Configure file permissions carefully, ensuring the container user only has access to necessary directories.

9.3.2 Encryption at Rest

- **Encrypted File Systems**: Set up host-level disk encryption for volumes containing sensitive data, especially if your host resides in a shared environment or is physically vulnerable.
- **Application-Level Encryption**: For databases, you might enable transparent data encryption or encrypt fields at the application layer.

9.3.3 Secrets Management

- **Don't Store Secrets in Volumes**: Avoid saving passwords, tokens, or certificates in Docker volumes unless necessary. Instead, use Docker Swarm/Kubernetes secrets or a dedicated secret manager (e.g., HashiCorp Vault, AWS Secrets Manager).
- **Rotate Credentials**: Regularly update passwords, API keys, and certificates. Stale credentials are a security liability.

9.3.4 Network Isolation

- **Limit Container Access**: If you're running a sensitive database container, restrict inbound connections to only the containers or networks that need them.
- **Firewall & IP Whitelisting**: Ensure your network configuration does not expose volumes or sensitive services to the public internet unintentionally.

9.4 Real-World Example: PostgreSQL with a Docker Volume and Restoring from Backup

Let's solidify these concepts by showing how to run a **PostgreSQL** container that uses a volume for data persistence, then restore it from a backup file.

9.4.1 Setting Up PostgreSQL with a Volume

1. **Create a Named Volume**:

   bash

   ```
   docker volume create pgdata
   ```

   This command registers a volume named **pgdata**. Docker will handle its storage location and lifecycle.

2. **Run PostgreSQL**:

   bash

   ```
   docker run -d \
     --name postgres-db \
     -e POSTGRES_PASSWORD=mysecretpassword \
     -v pgdata:/var/lib/postgresql/data \
     -p 5432:5432 \
     postgres:14
   ```

   o **-d**: Detaches and runs in the background.
   o **--name postgres-db**: Container name for easy reference.
   o **-e POSTGRES_PASSWORD=mysecretpasswor d**: Sets the default PostgreSQL superuser (postgres) password.

- o **-v pgdata:/var/lib/postgresql/data**: Mounts our named volume at the location where PostgreSQL stores its data files.
- o **-p 5432:5432**: Maps the container's port 5432 to port 5432 on the host.

3. **Verify**:
   - o Check logs to ensure PostgreSQL started without issues:

```bash

docker logs postgres-db
```

   - o You can connect to the database via `psql` on your host or a database client using `localhost:5432`, user `postgres`, password `mysecretpassword`.

9.4.2 Creating a Backup

Assume you have a database named `myappdb`. To create a dump file:

```bash

docker exec -it postgres-db \
  pg_dump -U postgres myappdb \
  > myappdb_backup.sql
```

- **docker exec**: Runs a command in an existing container.
- **-it**: Interactive terminal mode, so we can capture the output easily.
- **pg_dump**: PostgreSQL command for dumping databases.
- **> myappdb_backup.sql**: Redirects the output to a file on the host machine.

Now you have `myappdb_backup.sql` in your current directory on the **host**.

139

9.4.3 Restoring from a Backup

Let's simulate a scenario where we need to recover our database after removing the container.

1. **Remove the Existing Container** (if needed):

   bash

   ```
   docker stop postgres-db
   docker rm postgres-db
   ```

   Notice we did **not** remove the volume **pgdata**; you can keep it or create a new volume for a clean restore.

2. **Create a Fresh Container**:

   bash

   ```
   docker run -d \
     --name postgres-db-restore \
     -e POSTGRES_PASSWORD=newsecretpassword \
     -v pgdata:/var/lib/postgresql/data \
     -p 5432:5432 \
     postgres:14
   ```

   This starts a new container with the same volume. If you kept the old data in `pgdata`, your database is already there. If you want to restore from scratch, consider creating a new volume or manually clearing the old volume.

3. **Restore**:

   bash

   ```
   cat myappdb_backup.sql | docker exec -i
   postgres-db-restore \
    psql -U postgres -d myappdb
   ```

140

- o **cat myappdb_backup.sql**: Reads the backup file.
- o **docker exec -i**: Feeds the backup file contents into the container's stdin.
- o **psql -U postgres -d myappdb**: Tells PostgreSQL to restore the data into myappdb.

4. **Confirm the Data**:
   - o Connect to the newly restored database:

   ```bash
   docker exec -it postgres-db-restore
   psql -U postgres -d myappdb
   ```

   - o Check tables, rows, etc., to confirm the restore process succeeded.

9.4.4 Migrations

- • **To Another Host**:
  - o Use a tar-based or pg_dump approach.
  - o Transfer the backup file to the new host.
  - o Spin up a new PostgreSQL container and restore from that file.

Conclusion

Persisting data in Docker requires thoughtful planning— containers are ephemeral by design, so you must use **volumes** or **bind mounts** to save your application's crucial files. Docker volumes simplify storage management for production apps, while bind mounts are especially convenient for local development scenarios. Backups and migrations should be part of your standard workflow, ensuring that data can be recovered or moved without hiccups.

141

Security remains a top priority: run containers with the least privilege, use encryption where appropriate, and manage secrets responsibly to prevent unintended leaks. By adopting these best practices, you'll keep your data secure, maintain high availability, and reduce the operational headaches of manual interventions.

In the next chapter, **Chapter 10: Docker Networking Simplified**, we'll shift gears to explore how containers talk to each other and the outside world. You'll discover Docker's built-in network drivers, learn how to configure custom networks, and see how to secure container communication, rounding out your knowledge of Docker's core capabilities.

Key Takeaways

1. **Volumes vs. Bind Mounts**:
   - **Volumes** are managed by Docker, ideal for production data.
   - **Bind mounts** map host directories directly, great for development.
2. **Backups & Migrations**:
   - Use CLI commands (`tar`, `pg_dump`) or application-level tools.
   - Transfer volume archives or database dumps between hosts.
3. **Security Best Practices**:
   - Limit privileges, encrypt data at rest, and avoid storing secrets in volumes.
   - Restrict network access to sensitive containers.
4. **Real-World Example**:
   - PostgreSQL container with a named volume.
   - Backup using `pg_dump`, restore via `psql`.

- o This approach generalizes to other databases and applications.
5. **Data Persistence in Docker**:
   - o Containers are ephemeral, but data doesn't have to be.
   - o Plan your volume or bind mount strategy early to prevent data loss and ensure scalable, secure data management.

CHAPTER 10

Docker Networking Simplified

Introduction

Running applications in containers isn't just about packaging software—it also involves connecting those containers so they can communicate with each other and the outside world. Docker provides a robust, built-in networking model that abstracts away many low-level details, making it simpler to achieve secure and consistent networking configurations.

In this chapter, we'll break down Docker's primary **network drivers** (bridge, host, and none), walk through **creating custom networks**, and explain how **container-to-container communication** works under the hood. We'll then illustrate these principles with a real-world example of a multi-container environment—a simple web application talking to a database via a **custom bridge** network.

10.1 Why Docker Networking Matters

Before containers, your application might rely on the host's network stack or require complicated firewall rules and port mappings. Docker networking simplifies this by letting you create virtual networks that containers can join, ensuring they only communicate with the hosts or services you explicitly expose to them.

Benefits:

1. **Isolation**: Containers can remain invisible to external networks unless you choose to publish ports or connect them to specific networks.
2. **Port Management**: Avoid conflicts by assigning different internal ports to different containers, even if multiple services use the same external port mapping.
3. **Scalability**: Easily add or remove containers on the fly without manually editing network configurations.

10.2 Docker's Network Drivers

Docker includes several **network drivers**—each one sets up networking differently:

10.2.1 Bridge Network

- **Default Behavior**: When you run `docker run` without specifying a network, Docker typically places the container on a **bridge** network called `bridge` (on Linux).
- **What It Does**:
  - ○ Creates a virtual subnet and gateway for containers.
  - ○ Containers can communicate with each other on the same bridge network using their container names as hostnames.
- **Use Cases**:
  - ○ Local development or small-scale deployments where you need containers to talk to each other but you don't want them exposed to the outside world except through published ports.

10.2.2 Host Network

- **Definition**: Bypasses Docker's virtual network entirely and uses the **host's** networking stack.
- **Implications**:
  - A container on the host network uses the host's IP addresses and ports directly—no NAT (Network Address Translation) is set up by Docker.
  - This can lead to port conflicts if multiple containers listen on the same port.
- **Use Cases**:
  - Performance-sensitive applications that benefit from avoiding NAT overhead.
  - Situations where you need a container to listen on exactly the same IP/port as the host (e.g., a monitoring agent or a network tool).

10.2.3 None Network

- **Definition**: The container has **no** network interface aside from a **loopback** device.
- **Implications**:
  - The container cannot receive or send traffic beyond `localhost` inside its own namespace.
- **Use Cases**:
  - Extremely isolated or specialized workloads where external communication is undesirable.
  - Containers that run batch jobs or tasks with no network interaction.

10.2.4 Other Drivers

- **Overlay Networks**: Used with Docker Swarm or Kubernetes to connect containers across multiple hosts.
- **macvlan**: Assigns a unique MAC address and IP to the container on the local network, effectively making it appear as a separate physical device.

10.3 Creating Custom Networks

When you don't want to rely on the default `bridge` network, you can **create your own** bridge networks to group containers logically. This grants more control over IP ranges, DNS resolution, and access controls.

10.3.1 Steps to Create a Custom Bridge

1. **Create the Network**:

   ```bash
   docker network create \
     --driver bridge \
     --subnet 172.25.0.0/16 \
     my_custom_network
   ```

   - o **--driver bridge**: Specifies the network driver.
   - o **--subnet**: (Optional) Manually set an IP range for your network.

2. **Run Containers on the Network**:

   ```bash
   docker run -d \
     --name container1 \
     --network my_custom_network \
     someimage:latest
   ```

   This container now has an IP address on `my_custom_network` and can communicate with other containers that join the same network.

3. **Inspect the Network**:

   ```bash
   ```

```
docker network inspect my_custom_network
```

You'll see a JSON output listing connected containers, IP addresses, and additional details.

10.3.2 Advantages of Custom Networks

- **Container Name Resolution**: Docker automatically configures an internal DNS, so you can ping containers by name instead of IP.
- **Isolation**: Containers on one custom network are isolated from containers on another custom network unless explicitly connected.
- **Fine-Grained Control**: Configure subnets, gateways, or advanced policies as needed.

10.4 Container-to-Container Communication

When containers share the same **bridge network** (default or custom), they can communicate via **container names**. For example:

```bash
docker run -d --name app --network
my_custom_network app_image
docker run -d --name db --network
my_custom_network db_image
```

- **App** can reach **db** at http://db:<port> (if the DB exposes an HTTP interface), or db:<port> if it's a database service (like db:5432 for PostgreSQL).

10.4.1 Exposing vs. Publishing Ports

1. **Expose**:
   - o Defined in a Dockerfile using EXPOSE <port>.
   - o Simply indicates which ports the container *intends* to listen on.
   - o Doesn't make the port accessible outside the container unless it's on a shared network.
2. **Publish (Port Mapping)**:
   - o Achieved with -p <host_port>:<container_port> or --publish in the docker run command.
   - o Allows traffic from the host (or external networks) to reach the container.
   - o E.g., -p 8080:80 means the container's port 80 is mapped to host port 8080.

10.4.2 Linking Containers (Legacy Feature)

Docker links (using --link container_name:alias) is mostly superseded by Docker's **native DNS-based service discovery**. Linking is still supported, but best practice is to rely on custom networks for better flexibility and maintainability.

10.5 Real-World Example: Multi-Container Setup (Web + Database)

Let's walk through creating a basic web application (Node.js/Express) and a database (MySQL) that communicate on a **custom bridge** network.

10.5.1 Application Overview

1. **Web App** (Node.js + Express): Listens on port **3000**, connects to MySQL via hostname db on port ****3306\`**.

2. **Database** (MySQL): Runs on port **3306**, stores data for the web app.

10.5.2 Create the Custom Network

bash

```
docker network create \
  --driver bridge \
  my_app_network
```

10.5.3 Start the Database Container

bash

```
docker run -d \
  --name db \
  --network my_app_network \
  -e MYSQL_ROOT_PASSWORD=mysecret \
  -e MYSQL_DATABASE=myappdb \
  -e MYSQL_USER=myuser \
  -e MYSQL_PASSWORD=mypassword \
  mysql:8
```

- **-e** flags set environment variables recognized by the MySQL image (e.g., MYSQL_ROOT_PASSWORD).
- The container is attached to **my_app_network** with the name **db**.

10.5.4 Start the Web App Container

Assume we have a Docker image named **webapp:1.0** that expects:

- An environment variable DB_HOST to know where MySQL is.
- Port **3000** for HTTP requests.

bash

```
docker run -d \
  --name webapp \
  --network my_app_network \
  -e DB_HOST=db \
  -p 3000:3000 \
  webapp:1.0
```

- **-p 3000:3000** publishes the web app's container port 3000 to the host's port 3000.
- **-e DB_HOST=db** tells the web app to connect to the MySQL container at hostname **db** (which is automatically resolvable on the same network).

10.5.5 Verifying Communication

- **Check Container Logs**:

  ```bash
  bash
  ```

  ```
  docker logs db
  docker logs webapp
  ```

  Look for any connection success or error messages.

- **Access the Web App**:
  - Open your browser: **http://localhost:3000** (or the host's IP if remote).
  - The web app should respond, and any database operations will go to the **db** container.
- **Network Inspection**:

  ```bash
  bash
  ```

  ```
  docker network inspect my_app_network
  ```

  You'll see both webapp and db listed under **Containers**, each with an assigned IP address.

This setup demonstrates how containers interact behind the scenes without exposing the database to the public internet. Only the **webapp** container's port is published to the host, securing the database container by default.

Conclusion

Docker's networking model is both **powerful** and **user-friendly**. By providing different network drivers—bridge, host, none, and others—Docker covers a wide range of scenarios, from strict isolation to high-performance host networking. Creating **custom bridge networks** takes container isolation a step further, letting you define logical boundaries and easily reference containers by name.

In this chapter, we walked through container-to-container communication, clarifying the difference between **exposing** and **publishing** ports, and covered a real-world example in which a Node.js web app communicates with a MySQL database via a custom bridge network. This approach is foundational in microservice architectures, where each service lives in its own container or set of containers, all orchestrated through well-defined network topologies.

Next, in **Chapter 11: Docker Compose Essentials**, you'll learn how to automate multi-container setups using Docker Compose. Instead of running multiple `docker run` commands, you'll define your services in a single YAML file, streamlining how you configure networks, volumes, and dependencies for an entire application stack.

Key Takeaways

1. **Network Drivers**
   - **Bridge** (default): Containers communicate on a virtual subnet.
   - **Host**: Containers use the host's network stack directly.
   - **None**: Container has no external network access.
2. **Custom Bridge Networks**
   - Let you group containers, assign IP ranges, and enable DNS-based discovery by container name.
   - Improve isolation and simplify container-to-container communication.
3. **Container-to-Container Communication**
   - **Same Network**: Containers can talk to each other using container names as DNS hostnames.
   - **Published Ports**: Make a container's service available to the host or external clients.
4. **Real-World Example**
   - Web app + database on a custom bridge network.
   - The database is not publicly exposed; only the web app's port is mapped to the host.
5. **Security & Scalability**
   - Docker networking simplifies container communication while maintaining isolation.
   - You can scale services up or down without manually adjusting network configs, thanks to dynamic container service discovery.

PART III

Scaling and Orchestration

CHAPTER 11

Docker Compose Essentials

Introduction

As you move beyond single-container setups, you'll often need to manage multiple containers at once—perhaps a web server, a database, a caching layer, and more. While running each container manually is doable, it quickly becomes cumbersome. Enter **Docker Compose**, a command-line tool and file format designed for defining and running multi-container Docker applications with minimal fuss.

With Docker Compose, you describe your entire stack—containers, networks, volumes, environment variables—using a simple YAML file. A single command can then build and start all the services you need. This approach is invaluable for local development, where developers frequently spin up and tear down environments as they code, test, and iterate. Compose is also used in some production scenarios—though for larger-scale deployments, you might eventually transition to orchestration systems like Kubernetes or Docker Swarm. Nonetheless, Docker Compose remains a foundational tool in many development workflows.

11.1 What Is Docker Compose?

Docker Compose is a separate but closely related tool to Docker itself. You can think of Compose as a way to:

155

1. **Define** all your application's services in a single YAML file (by default named `docker-compose.yml`).
2. **Start** all those services with a single command: `docker-compose up`.
3. **Manage** them collectively—stopping, removing, and inspecting multiple containers at once.

Why Compose Matters:

- **Consistency**: Every developer or team member runs the same environment.
- **Simplicity**: One YAML file describes the entire stack; no need to memorize long `docker run` commands.
- **Modularity**: Easily attach or remove components (services, volumes, networks) without rewriting large amounts of configuration.

11.2 Docker Compose File Structure

A typical Docker Compose file (named `docker-compose.yml`) starts with a **version** (Compose file format), followed by **services**. You can also define **volumes**, **networks**, and advanced configurations like environment variables or build contexts.

Here's a minimal example:

```yaml
version: '3.9'     # Specifies the Compose file
format version

services:
  web:
    image: nginx:latest
    ports:
      - "80:80"
```

```
    volumes:
      - ./html:/usr/share/nginx/html:ro
    networks:
      - myapp-net

  database:
    image: mysql:8
    environment:
      - MYSQL_ROOT_PASSWORD=secret
      - MYSQL_DATABASE=myappdb
    volumes:
      - dbdata:/var/lib/mysql
    networks:
      - myapp-net

volumes:
  dbdata:

networks:
  myapp-net:
    driver: bridge
```

11.2.1 version

- **version**: **'3.9'**: Indicates which Compose features are supported. The 3.x series is widely used and compatible with current Docker Engine releases.
- Different Compose versions can include additional features or syntax, but the fundamental structure remains consistent.

11.2.2 services

- **services**:: Defines each container you want to run as part of your application stack.

web example:

- **image**: **nginx**:**latest**: We're using the official Nginx image.

157

- **ports**:: Maps port 80 on the container to port 80 on the host.
- **volumes**:: Binds the local `./html` directory to the container's `/usr/share/nginx/html` directory as read-only (`:ro`).
- **networks**:: Specifies that this service joins the network **myapp-net**.

database example:

- **image: mysql:8**: Pulls the official MySQL 8 image.
- **environment**:: Defines environment variables recognized by the MySQL image.
- **volumes**:: Attaches the named volume **dbdata** to `/var/lib/mysql`.
- **networks**:: Also connected to **myapp-net** so `web` can communicate with `database`.

11.2.3 volumes

- **volumes**:: Declares named volumes for persistent storage. In the example, **dbdata** is used by the database container.
- Once declared, these volumes can be referenced by any service in the `services` section.

11.2.4 networks

- **networks**:: Docker Compose lets you define custom networks (like **myapp-net**) to isolate services.
- **driver: bridge**: Uses Docker's default bridge driver, allowing internal DNS resolution so containers can talk to each other by name (e.g., `database`).

11.3 Common Docker Compose Commands

11.3.1 docker-compose up

- **Purpose**: Builds and starts all services in the docker-compose.yml.
- **Usage**:

```bash

docker-compose up
```

By default, Compose runs in the foreground, showing logs for all services in the terminal.

- **Flags**:
  - -**d** (detached): Runs services in the background.
  - --**build**: Forces a rebuild of images before starting.

11.3.2 docker-compose down

- **Purpose**: Stops and removes containers, networks, and (optionally) volumes created by docker-compose up.
- **Usage**:

```bash

docker-compose down
```

- **Flags**:
  - -**v**: Remove named volumes declared in the YAML.
  - --**rmi all**: Remove all images used by the Compose file (be careful!).

11.3.3 docker-compose logs

159

- **Purpose**: Fetches logs from running services.
- **Usage**:

```bash
docker-compose logs
```

Prints logs for all containers. You can specify a particular service:

```bash
docker-compose logs web
```

- **Flags**:
  - o **-f** (follow): Continues streaming new log output in real time.

11.3.4 docker-compose ps

- **Purpose**: Lists containers managed by Docker Compose.
- **Usage**:

```bash
docker-compose ps
```

- **Displays**: Container names, command, state, ports, and more, letting you quickly see which services are up or down.

11.4 Local Development Workflows with Docker Compose

11.4.1 Setting Up a Dev Environment

160

Compose is especially handy for local development because you can easily spin up a suite of services. For instance, if your application depends on a web server, a database, and a caching service (like Redis), you can define all these in a single YAML file. Then:

1. **Run**:

   ```bash
   docker-compose up -d
   ```

   All services start in the background.

2. **Update Code**: If you're using bind mounts or rebuilding images, you can quickly reflect code changes without manual container restarts.
3. **Shutdown**:

   ```bash
   docker-compose down
   ```

   A single command tears down the environment when you're done.

11.4.2   Overriding   with   docker-compose.override.yml

Compose supports an **override** file—docker-compose.override.yml—which merges with your main docker-compose.yml. This is a powerful way to tweak configurations for local development without changing production settings. For example, you might mount local source code, enable debugging tools, or vary environment variables.

11.5 Real-World Example: LAMP/LEMP Stack for a Small Team

A classic use case for Docker Compose is building and testing a **LAMP** (Linux, Apache, MySQL, PHP) or **LEMP** (Linux, Nginx, MySQL, PHP) stack. Let's illustrate how a small team might collaborate using a Compose file that sets up a simple LEMP environment.

11.5.1 File Structure

Assume a project directory like:

```
css
```

```
my-website/
   ├── docker-compose.yml
   ├── src/
   │    └── index.php
   └── nginx.conf
```

- **src/**: Contains PHP files.
- **nginx.conf**: Custom Nginx configuration file.
- **docker-compose.yml**: Defines our multi-container setup.

11.5.2 docker-compose.yml

```yaml
version: '3.9'

services:
  web:
    image: nginx:latest
    container_name: my-web
```

```
volumes:
  - ./src:/var/www/html
  - ./nginx.conf:/etc/nginx/nginx.conf:ro
ports:
  - "8080:80"
depends_on:
  - php
networks:
  - webnet

php:
  image: php:8-fpm
  container_name: my-php
  volumes:
    - ./src:/var/www/html
  networks:
    - webnet

db:
  image: mysql:5.7
  container_name: my-db
  environment:
    MYSQL_ROOT_PASSWORD: example
    MYSQL_DATABASE: mydb
    MYSQL_USER: myuser
    MYSQL_PASSWORD: mypass
  volumes:
    - dbdata:/var/lib/mysql
  networks:
    - webnet

volumes:
  dbdata:

networks:
  webnet:
    driver: bridge
```

Explanation

1. **web** (Nginx Container)
   o Mounts ./src to /var/www/html, so any PHP files are served by Nginx.

163

- o Uses a custom `nginx.conf` to configure server blocks or PHP-FPM upstream settings.
- o Publishes container's port 80 to host's port **8080**.
- o Depends on `php` to ensure the PHP container starts before it tries to proxy requests.

2. **php** (PHP-FPM Container)
   - o Uses the **php:8-fpm** image with FastCGI Process Manager (FPM).
   - o Shares the `./src` directory, so Nginx and PHP reference the same code.

3. **db** (MySQL Container)
   - o Sets environment variables for MySQL credentials.
   - o Stores data in a named volume **dbdata** for persistence.

4. **networks**
   - o **webnet** is a custom bridge, allowing the containers to resolve each other by name (`web`, `php`, `db`) and communicate internally.

5. **volumes**
   - o **dbdata** is a named volume for MySQL data.

11.5.3 Starting the Stack

From the **my-website** directory:

```bash
```

```bash
docker-compose up -d
```

Compose pulls the images (Nginx, PHP-FPM, MySQL), creates volumes, sets up a bridge network, and runs all containers in the background.

Check:

```bash
```

```
docker-compose ps
```

You should see all three services (`my-web`, `my-php`, `my-db`) running. Then go to `http://localhost:8080` in your browser. You'll see your site's index page, rendered through PHP-FPM and served by Nginx. The site can also connect to the MySQL database as needed.

11.5.4 Logs and Updates

- **View Logs**:

    ```
    bash

    docker-compose logs -f
    ```

    Shows combined logs from web, php, and db.

- **Modifying Code**:
    - o Any changes to **src/** files take effect immediately because of the bind mount.
- **Stopping the Stack**:

    ```
    bash

    docker-compose down
    ```

    Safely stops containers and (unless specified) preserves named volumes for persistent data.

11.5.5 Team Collaboration

Version Control: Your `docker-compose.yml`, `nginx.conf`, and `src` files are committed to a Git repository. Each team member can clone the repo, run `docker-compose up -d`, and get the exact same environment—eliminating the "works on my machine" problem.

165

Conclusion

Docker Compose streamlines the process of defining and running multi-container applications, making it a go-to solution for local development and smaller-scale production setups. By consolidating your environment configuration into a single `docker-compose.yml` file, you reduce the complexity of managing multiple `docker run` commands and ensure consistency across team members or environments.

In this chapter, we covered the basics of Compose file structure (services, volumes, networks), explored the essential commands (`up`, `down`, `logs`, `ps`), and saw how to integrate these concepts into everyday development workflows. Our real-world LAMP/LEMP example demonstrated how a small team could easily collaborate on a project running Nginx, PHP-FPM, and MySQL containers.

Next, in **Chapter 12: Advanced Docker Compose and Configuration**, we'll dive deeper into Compose's more sophisticated features—such as environment variable usage, multi-file Compose setups, and overriding configurations for different environments. You'll also learn about more advanced networking strategies and how to apply best practices for a smoother developer experience.

Key Takeaways

1. **Docker Compose**: A tool for defining and running multi-container Docker applications with a simple YAML file.
2. **Compose File Structure**:

- o **services** define containers,
- o **volumes** declare storage, and
- o **networks** create custom communication layers.

3. **Common Commands**:
- o `docker-compose up`: Start all services,
- o `docker-compose down`: Stop and remove containers,
- o `logs`, `ps`, and more to monitor and manage.

4. **Local Development Workflow**:
- o Compose is excellent for spinning up consistent dev environments.
- o Use override files for environment-specific tweaks.

5. **Real-World Example**:
- o A LEMP stack (Nginx, PHP, MySQL) with Docker Compose, easily shared among teammates.
- o Named volumes persist data, bind mounts allow live code edits, and a custom network ties it all together.

CHAPTER 12

Advanced Docker Compose and Configuration

Introduction

Docker Compose has proven invaluable for orchestrating multi-container applications in development. As your projects grow in complexity, you'll often need more than a single, static `docker-compose.yml` file to manage differing requirements across environments. In this chapter, we dive into advanced configuration patterns that let you tailor your Compose setup to various stages of your application lifecycle—from local development and testing to staging and production.

We'll begin by exploring how to use environment variables to inject configuration dynamically into your Compose files. Next, we'll discuss techniques for overriding and extending Compose configurations to create distinct setups for dev, staging, and production environments. Finally, we'll touch on advanced networking strategies that allow for robust container communication in complex applications. A detailed real-world example will show you how a microservice system can be configured using separate Compose files to meet different deployment needs.

12.1 Environment Variable Usage

12.1.1 Why Use Environment Variables?

Environment variables in Docker Compose allow you to parameterize your configurations so that you don't have to hardcode sensitive or environment-specific details (such as API endpoints, database credentials, or service URLs) into your Compose file. This approach improves security and flexibility. For example, the same service definition can point to a local database in development or a managed database service in production simply by changing environment variables.

12.1.2 Techniques for Injecting Environment Variables

- **Inline in the Compose File**: In the `environment:` section of a service, you can define variables directly:

```yaml
services:
  app:
    image: myapp:latest
    environment:
      - APP_ENV=production
      - API_URL=https://api.mycompany.com
```

- **Using a .env File**: Docker Compose automatically reads a file named `.env` in the same directory as your Compose file. This file can store key-value pairs:

```dotenv
```

```
APP_ENV=development
API_URL=http://localhost:3000
```

Then, in your Compose file, you can reference these variables:

```
yaml

services:
  app:
    image: myapp:latest
    environment:
      - APP_ENV=${APP_ENV}
      - API_URL=${API_URL}
```

- **Command-Line   Overrides**: You can also override environment variables when running Compose:

```
bash

API_URL=https://staging.api.mycompany.com
docker-compose up -d
```

12.1.3 Best Practices

- **Keep Secrets Secure**: Never store sensitive credentials directly in your Compose file or commit them to version control. Use secret management tools (e.g., Docker secrets, HashiCorp Vault) or environment-specific .env files that are excluded from version control.
- **Document Variables**: Include comments or documentation to explain the purpose of each environment variable, especially if multiple developers will use the same configuration.

12.2 Overriding Configurations for Different Environments

12.2.1 Why Override?

Different environments (development, staging, production) often require different settings. For instance, you might want to mount local volumes and enable debugging in development, but use optimized images and stricter settings in production. Overriding allows you to maintain a base Compose file while selectively modifying parameters for each environment.

12.2.2 Techniques for Overriding Configurations

*   **Multiple Compose Files**: Docker Compose supports merging multiple YAML files. You can have a base file (e.g., `docker-compose.yml`) and an override file (e.g., `docker-compose.override.yml` or `docker-compose.prod.yml`).

    Base File (`docker-compose.yml`):

    ```yaml
    yaml

    version: '3.9'

    services:
      serviceA:
        image: servicea:latest
        environment:
          - API_URL=${API_URL}
        networks:
          - backend

    networks:
    ```

171

```
backend:
  driver: bridge
```

Development Override (docker-compose.override.yml):

yaml

```
version: '3.9'

services:
  serviceA:
    build: ./serviceA
    environment:
      - API_URL=http://localhost:8080
    volumes:
      - ./serviceA/src:/app/src
```

Production Override (docker-compose.prod.yml):

yaml

```
version: '3.9'

services:
  serviceA:
    image: servicea:stable
    environment:
      - API_URL=https://api.mycompany.com
```

When starting your containers, you can specify which files to merge:

bash

```
# For development (default files are
docker-compose.yml + docker-
compose.override.yml)
docker-compose up -d
```

```
# For production:
docker-compose  -f  docker-compose.yml  -f
docker-compose.prod.yml up -d
```

- **Using   Profiles**:
  Compose profiles allow you to selectively enable
  services. For instance:

```
yaml

services:
  debug-service:
    image: debug-tool:latest
    profiles: ["dev"]
```

Then run:

```
bash

docker-compose --profile dev up -d
```

12.2.3 Best Practices

- **Keep Base Files Generic**: Your base Compose file
  should define the core services and settings.
  Environment-specific overrides should only change
  what's necessary.
- **Version Control**: Maintain separate override files for
  each environment in your repository, so team members
  can see the differences.
- **Document Usage**: Provide clear instructions (in a
  README or similar) on how to launch the appropriate
  configuration for each environment.

12.3 Docker Compose Networking in Complex Applications

12.3.1 Networking Beyond the Basics

While earlier chapters covered creating custom networks, complex applications may require more nuanced network configurations:

- **Multiple Networks**: Different services might need to communicate only within certain groups. For example, a microservice might expose one network for external communication and another for internal service-to-service communication.
- **Network Isolation and Segmentation**: This helps to increase security by limiting exposure and simplifying firewall rules.

12.3.2 Configuring Multiple Networks

In your Compose file, you can define multiple networks and assign services to one or more of them. For example:

```yaml
version: '3.9'

services:
  frontend:
    image: frontend:latest
    networks:
      - public_net
      - internal_net

  backend:
    image: backend:latest
    networks:
      - internal_net
```

```
networks:
  public_net:
    driver: bridge
  internal_net:
    driver: bridge
```

In this configuration:

- The **frontend** service is accessible on both the public and internal networks.
- The **backend** service is only available on the internal network, limiting its exposure.

12.3.3 Best Practices

- **Define Clear Network Boundaries**: Document which services belong to which networks and why.
- **Use DNS Resolution**: Rely on Docker's built-in DNS to refer to services by name within networks, reducing the need for static IP configurations.

12.4 Real-World Example: Setting Up Separate Compose Files for a Microservice System

Imagine you're building a microservice-based system that includes several services (e.g., user service, payment service, and notification service). Your team needs different configurations for local development, testing, and production.

12.4.1 Base Compose File (docker-compose.yml)

This file defines the core services and shared networks:

yaml

```
version: '3.9'

services:
  user-service:
    image: user-service:latest
    environment:
      - SERVICE_PORT=5001
    networks:
      - micro_net

  payment-service:
    image: payment-service:latest
    environment:
      - SERVICE_PORT=5002
    networks:
      - micro_net

  notification-service:
    image: notification-service:latest
    environment:
      - SERVICE_PORT=5003
    networks:
      - micro_net

networks:
  micro_net:
    driver: bridge
```

12.4.2 Development Override (docker-compose.override.yml)

For local development, you may need to build images from source, mount local directories for live code editing, and use different environment variables:

```yaml
version: '3.9'

services:
  user-service:
```

```
build: ./user-service
volumes:
  - ./user-service/src:/app/src
environment:
  - SERVICE_PORT=5001
  - API_ENDPOINT=http://localhost:3000

payment-service:
  build: ./payment-service
  volumes:
    - ./payment-service/src:/app/src
  environment:
    - SERVICE_PORT=5002
    - PAYMENT_MODE=dev

notification-service:
  build: ./notification-service
  volumes:
    - ./notification-service/src:/app/src
  environment:
    - SERVICE_PORT=5003
    - NOTIFY_MODE=dev
```

12.4.3 Production Override (docker-compose.prod.yml)

For production, you'll use pre-built images from your registry, different environment settings, and possibly enhanced security configurations:

yaml

```
version: '3.9'

services:
  user-service:
    image: myregistry.com/user-service:stable
    environment:
      - SERVICE_PORT=5001
      - API_ENDPOINT=https://api.mycompany.com

  payment-service:
```

```
image: myregistry.com/payment-service:stable
environment:
    - SERVICE_PORT=5002
    - PAYMENT_MODE=prod

notification-service:
    image:         myregistry.com/notification-
service:stable
    environment:
        - SERVICE_PORT=5003
        - NOTIFY_MODE=prod
```

12.4.4 Running the System

- **Local   Development**:
  Simply run:

  ```
  bash

  docker-compose up -d
  ```

  Docker Compose automatically merges `docker-compose.yml` **with** `docker-compose.override.yml`, giving you a development-friendly environment with live code mounts and local build instructions.

- **Production   Deployment**:
  When deploying to production, you would use:

  ```
  bash

  docker-compose  -f  docker-compose.yml  -f
  docker-compose.prod.yml up -d
  ```

  This command merges the base configuration with the production-specific overrides, ensuring your services run with the correct images and environment settings.

Conclusion

Advanced Docker Compose configurations enable you to tailor your container orchestration to the specific needs of different environments. By leveraging environment variables, you can inject dynamic configuration into your services. Overriding configurations with multiple Compose files or profiles allows you to maintain a single source of truth while adjusting settings for development, testing, or production. Furthermore, understanding complex networking setups—such as using multiple networks for service isolation—ensures that your microservices can communicate securely and efficiently.

In this chapter, you learned practical techniques to manage these advanced scenarios. The real-world example of a microservice system with separate Compose files illustrates how to seamlessly transition from local development to production without rewriting configurations.

As you integrate these practices into your workflow, you'll find that Docker Compose not only simplifies multi-container management but also provides the flexibility needed to support diverse deployment strategies.

Key Takeaways

1. **Environment Variables**:
   o Use inline definitions, a .env file, or command-line overrides to inject configuration dynamically.
2. **Overriding Configurations**:

    o   Maintain a base Compose file and use additional override files (e.g., `docker-compose.override.yml`, `docker-compose.prod.yml`) to tailor settings for different environments.

3. **Advanced Networking**:
    o   Design custom network topologies with multiple networks to isolate and manage inter-service communication.

4. **Real-World Example**:
    o   Separate Compose files for a microservice system enable consistent development, testing, and production environments without duplicating configuration.

5. **Best Practices**:
    o   Keep sensitive data secure, document your variables, and maintain clear version control of your Compose files.

CHAPTER 13

Docker Swarm: Native Container Orchestration

Introduction

As your containerized applications grow and demand higher availability, you need a robust orchestration system to manage, scale, and load balance your services. **Docker Swarm** is Docker's native clustering and orchestration tool that turns a pool of Docker hosts into a single, virtual Docker Engine. With Swarm, you can deploy services across multiple nodes, manage service replicas, and distribute network traffic automatically. In this chapter, we'll walk through the process of initializing a Swarm cluster, deploying services and stacks, and scaling containers efficiently. We'll also provide a real-world example that converts a Docker Compose setup into a Swarm stack suitable for handling production workloads.

13.1 Initializing a Swarm Cluster

13.1.1 What Is Docker Swarm?

Docker Swarm allows you to group multiple Docker hosts (nodes) into a single cluster with one unified interface. Within this cluster, you can deploy services that are automatically distributed and load balanced across the nodes.

13.1.2 Setting Up Your First Swarm

To get started, you need to initialize the Swarm mode on your Docker host. On a single node (ideal for testing and development), run:

```bash
docker swarm init
```

- **Output** **Example**:
  Swarm mode is now active on this node. Docker displays a join token and the manager's IP address, which you can use to add more worker or manager nodes to your Swarm cluster.

If you plan to add additional nodes, follow the instructions provided by the output (using `docker swarm join ...` on the other hosts). This simple command transforms a standalone Docker Engine into a Swarm manager, ready to orchestrate services across the cluster.

13.2 Managing Services and Stacks

13.2.1 Services: The Building Blocks

In Swarm mode, you don't run individual containers directly. Instead, you deploy **services** that define a desired state (e.g., number of replicas) and the image to use. Docker Swarm ensures that this state is maintained by creating and managing container replicas automatically.

- **Creating a Service**:

```bash
```

```
docker service create --name webapp --
publish 80:80 nginx:latest
```

This command creates a service named webapp using the nginx:latest image and publishes port 80 on the host.

- **Listing Services**:

```bash
docker service ls
```

- **Inspecting a Service**:

```bash
docker service ps webapp
```

This displays the status and distribution of the service's tasks (container replicas) across the cluster.

13.2.2 Stacks: Grouping Multiple Services

A **stack** in Docker Swarm allows you to deploy multiple interrelated services defined in a Compose file. Stacks enable you to manage a complete multi-container application with one command.

- **Deploying a Stack**:

```bash
docker stack deploy -c docker-compose.yml my_stack
```

183

This command reads the Compose file (docker-compose.yml) and deploys the defined services as a stack named my_stack. Docker Swarm then manages service replication, networking, and load balancing across the nodes.

13.3 Scaling Containers and Load Balancing

13.3.1 Scaling Services

One of Swarm's key strengths is its ability to scale services seamlessly. You can increase or decrease the number of replicas for a given service without downtime.

- **Scaling a Service**:

    ```bash
    docker service scale webapp=5
    ```

    This command scales the webapp service to 5 replicas. Docker Swarm automatically distributes these replicas across available nodes.

13.3.2 Built-In Load Balancing

Docker Swarm includes built-in load balancing. When a service is scaled, incoming requests are distributed evenly among all replicas. This ensures that no single container becomes a bottleneck and that the load is managed efficiently, improving overall application performance and availability.

13.4 Real-World Example: Converting a Docker Compose Setup into a Docker Swarm Stack

Imagine you have a Docker Compose file for a simple web application that includes a web server and a database. In development, you might use Compose to spin up these containers on a single machine. Now, to handle heavier production loads, you can convert this Compose setup into a Docker Swarm stack.

13.4.1 Original Docker Compose File (docker-compose.yml)

```yaml
yaml

version: '3.9'

services:
  web:
    image: my-webapp:latest
    ports:
      - "80:80"
    depends_on:
      - db

  db:
    image: mysql:5.7
    environment:
      MYSQL_ROOT_PASSWORD: example
    volumes:
      - dbdata:/var/lib/mysql

volumes:
  dbdata:
```

13.4.2 Converting to a Swarm Stack

1. **Initialize Swarm Mode**:
Ensure that Swarm is initialized on your production node:

bash

```
docker swarm init
```

2. **Deploy the Stack**:
Use the same Compose file to deploy the stack:

bash

```
docker stack deploy -c docker-compose.yml
production_stack
```

Docker Swarm will interpret the Compose file, create services for web and db, and automatically distribute the web service's containers (replicas) across the cluster.

3. **Scale the Web Service**:
To handle increased load, scale the web service:

bash

```
docker                service                scale
production_stack_web=10
```

This command increases the number of web replicas to 10. Swarm's load balancer will distribute incoming requests evenly among them.

4. **Monitoring and Management**:
   o **List Services**:

   bash

```
docker service ls
```

o **Inspect Service Tasks**:

```
bash
```

```
docker          service          ps
production_stack_web
```

5. With these commands, you can verify that your services are distributed as expected and that your application is ready to handle a heavier load.

Conclusion

Docker Swarm provides a native, integrated way to orchestrate and scale containerized applications. By initializing a Swarm cluster, you can deploy services and stacks that are automatically load balanced across multiple nodes. The ability to scale services seamlessly—combined with built-in load balancing—makes Swarm an ideal solution for production environments that need to handle fluctuating traffic loads.

In this chapter, we explored how to initialize a Swarm cluster, manage services and stacks, and scale containers to meet production demands. Our real-world example demonstrated the conversion of a Docker Compose setup into a Swarm stack, providing a practical workflow for transitioning from development to production in a scalable manner.

Key Takeaways

1. **Swarm Initialization**:
   - Use `docker swarm init` to start a Swarm cluster and transform a single Docker host into a cluster manager.
2. **Managing Services and Stacks**:
   - Services are the building blocks in Swarm; stacks group related services defined in a Compose file.
3. **Scaling and Load Balancing**:
   - Scale services using `docker service scale` and rely on built-in load balancing to distribute traffic evenly.
4. **Real-World Conversion**:
   - Transition a Docker Compose setup into a Swarm stack using `docker stack deploy` to handle production-level traffic.
5. **Production Readiness**:
   - Docker Swarm's native orchestration enables automated service replication, efficient resource use, and high availability in multi-node clusters.

CHAPTER 14

Kubernetes vs. Docker Swarm

Introduction

As organizations scale their containerized applications, the need for robust orchestration becomes paramount. Two of the most popular solutions are **Docker Swarm** and **Kubernetes**. Both enable you to manage and deploy containers across clusters of machines, but they approach orchestration in fundamentally different ways. This chapter compares the two platforms, examines key Kubernetes concepts such as Pods, Deployments, and Services, and weighs the pros and cons of each approach. We also explore hybrid solutions like Docker Desktop's integrated Kubernetes option and walk through a real-world example of migrating a small application from Docker Swarm to Kubernetes.

14.1 Key Kubernetes Concepts

Pods

- **Definition**: In Kubernetes, a **Pod** is the smallest deployable unit. A Pod can contain one or more containers that share storage, network, and specification for how to run.
- **Purpose**: Pods provide a higher level of abstraction than individual containers by grouping them together. This

grouping enables shared resources and ensures that tightly coupled containers run on the same node.

Deployments

- **Definition**: A **Deployment** is a higher-level abstraction that defines the desired state for your application, such as the number of Pod replicas and the update strategy.
- **Purpose**: Deployments manage the lifecycle of Pods, handle rolling updates, and ensure that the desired number of replicas is always running. They also provide self-healing by automatically replacing failed Pods.

Services

- **Definition**: A **Service** in Kubernetes is an abstraction that defines a logical set of Pods and a policy by which to access them.
- **Purpose**: Services provide stable network endpoints and load balancing, ensuring that even as Pods come and go, your application remains accessible under a consistent address.

14.2 Docker Swarm Overview

Docker Swarm is Docker's native orchestration tool. It offers a simpler, more integrated experience with Docker's ecosystem. With Swarm, you deploy services (groups of containers) and manage their scaling, load balancing, and health—all through familiar Docker commands. Although it is easier to set up and use, Swarm is generally considered less feature-rich and flexible than Kubernetes, especially as applications become more complex.

14.3 Pros and Cons: Docker Swarm vs. Kubernetes

Docker Swarm

Pros:

- **Simplicity**: Integrated with Docker CLI, making it easier for teams already familiar with Docker.
- **Quick Setup**: Swarm mode can be initialized with a single command (`docker swarm init`).
- **Seamless Integration**: Works well out-of-the-box with existing Docker tools and Compose files.

Cons:

- **Limited Feature Set**: Lacks some of the advanced scheduling and self-healing capabilities offered by Kubernetes.
- **Scalability Constraints**: Although suitable for many use cases, Swarm may struggle with extremely large or complex deployments.
- **Smaller Ecosystem**: Fewer community resources and third-party integrations compared to Kubernetes.

Kubernetes

Pros:

- **Robustness**: Offers extensive features such as auto-scaling, advanced health checks, and a rich ecosystem of plugins.
- **Flexibility**: Provides fine-grained control over scheduling, networking, and security policies.
- **Community and Ecosystem**: A large, active community with numerous tools, extensions, and cloud provider integrations.

Cons:

- **Complexity**: Steeper learning curve due to its many abstractions and configuration options.
- **Resource Intensive**: Typically requires more resources and a more complex setup compared to Docker Swarm.
- **Management Overhead**: Maintaining a Kubernetes cluster can be challenging without proper tooling and expertise.

14.4 Hybrid Approaches: Docker Desktop's Kubernetes Integration

To bridge the gap between simplicity and advanced orchestration, Docker Desktop now includes built-in Kubernetes support. This hybrid approach allows developers to experiment with Kubernetes on their local machines without needing to set up a separate cluster. It offers the best of both worlds: the ease of Docker Swarm for simple tasks and the power of Kubernetes when advanced orchestration is required.

14.5 Real-World Example: Migrating from Docker Swarm to Kubernetes

Imagine you have a small web application that has been running on Docker Swarm. Your Docker Compose file has been deployed as a Swarm stack to manage a service with a simple load-balanced web server and a database. As traffic increases, you decide to migrate the application to Kubernetes for its enhanced scalability and advanced scheduling features.

Migration Steps:

1. **Preparation**:
   o **Assess Your Current Setup**: Review your Docker Compose file used in Swarm. Identify the services, environment variables, and volume mounts.
   o **Install Kubernetes**: Set up a Kubernetes cluster (using tools like Minikube for local testing or a managed service such as GKE, EKS, or AKS for production).
2. **Translate Docker Compose to Kubernetes Manifests**:
   o **Pods/Deployments**: Convert your service definitions into Kubernetes Deployments. For example, your web server becomes a Deployment with a defined number of replicas.
   o **Services**: Create Kubernetes Service resources to provide stable endpoints and load balancing for your Deployments.
   o **Volumes**: Map your Docker volumes to Kubernetes PersistentVolumeClaims for data persistence.
3. **Example Conversion**:
   o **Docker Swarm (Docker Compose snippet)**:

```yaml
services:
  web:
    image: my-webapp:latest
    ports:
      - "80:80"
    deploy:
      replicas: 3
  db:
    image: mysql:5.7
    environment:
      MYSQL_ROOT_PASSWORD: example
    volumes:
```

```
      - dbdata:/var/lib/mysql
volumes:
  dbdata:
```

- o **Kubernetes Manifests**:
  - **Deployment for Web App** (web-deployment.yaml):

    yaml

    ```
    apiVersion: apps/v1
    kind: Deployment
    metadata:
      name: webapp
    spec:
      replicas: 3
      selector:
        matchLabels:
          app: webapp
      template:
        metadata:
          labels:
            app: webapp
        spec:
          containers:
          - name: webapp
            image:            my-
    webapp:latest
            ports:
            - containerPort: 80
    ```

  - **Service for Web App** (web-service.yaml):

    yaml

    ```
    apiVersion: v1
    kind: Service
    metadata:
      name: webapp-service
    spec:
      selector:
    ```

194

```
      app: webapp
    ports:
    - protocol: TCP
      port: 80
      targetPort: 80
    type: LoadBalancer
```

- **Deployment for Database** and **PersistentVolumeClaim** follow similar patterns.

4. **Deployment and Testing**:
   o Apply your manifests:

   ```bash
   kubectl apply -f web-deployment.yaml
   kubectl apply -f web-service.yaml
   # And similarly for the database and
   its storage
   ```

   o Verify that the Pods are running and the Service is exposing your web application.

5. **Differences in Setup and Maintenance**:
   o **Setup Complexity**: Kubernetes requires writing multiple YAML files for each resource, whereas Docker Swarm can deploy a single stack file.
   o **Maintenance**: Kubernetes offers advanced features like rolling updates and self-healing, but it demands more monitoring and configuration management.
   o **Tooling**: Kubernetes benefits from a rich ecosystem (kubectl, Helm, etc.), but managing these tools can add overhead.

Conclusion

Both Docker Swarm and Kubernetes provide powerful solutions for container orchestration, yet they cater to different needs. Docker Swarm offers simplicity and ease of use for smaller or less complex environments, while Kubernetes delivers advanced features and scalability for large-scale, dynamic deployments. In this chapter, we explored the fundamental Kubernetes concepts of Pods, Deployments, and Services, compared the two orchestration platforms, and discussed hybrid approaches such as Docker Desktop's Kubernetes integration. The migration example illustrates real-world considerations when moving from a Docker Swarm setup to Kubernetes, emphasizing differences in configuration, management, and operational complexity.

Key Takeaways

1. **Core Concepts**:
   o Kubernetes uses Pods, Deployments, and Services to manage containerized applications, while Docker Swarm relies on services and stacks.
2. **Pros and Cons**:
   o Docker Swarm is simpler to set up and integrates well with Docker tools but lacks some of the advanced features found in Kubernetes.
   o Kubernetes offers robust scalability and a rich ecosystem, albeit with greater complexity and resource requirements.
3. **Hybrid Approaches**:
   o Tools like Docker Desktop allow you to run Kubernetes locally, blending the benefits of both orchestration systems.
4. **Real-World Migration**:
   o Transitioning from Docker Swarm to Kubernetes involves converting a single Docker Compose file into multiple Kubernetes manifests, resulting

in a more granular control over deployment and maintenance.

5. **Choosing the Right Tool**:
   o Your choice depends on your project's scale, complexity, and operational requirements; smaller teams might favor Docker Swarm, while larger, dynamic environments benefit from Kubernetes.

PART IV

Security, Performance, and Reliability

CHAPTER 15

Container Security Fundamentals

Introduction

As containerized applications become a core part of modern software deployments, securing these containers is critical. Container security spans multiple layers—from ensuring that base images are free of vulnerabilities to enforcing strict runtime policies. In this chapter, we introduce best practices for securing containers at every stage of their lifecycle. We cover techniques for scanning images for known vulnerabilities and malware, discuss the importance of running containers as non-root users, and explore methods for managing sensitive data such as API keys and credentials. These practices not only protect your applications but also help build trust in your containerized infrastructure.

15.1 Image Scanning: Detecting Vulnerabilities and Malware

15.1.1 Why Image Scanning Matters

Before you deploy any container, it's essential to ensure that the underlying image does not contain known security vulnerabilities or malware. Since container images often include operating system packages, libraries, and third-party software, they can be susceptible to security issues that, if left unaddressed, might expose your applications to attacks.

15.1.2 Tools and Techniques

Several tools can help you scan container images:

- **Trivy**: An open-source vulnerability scanner that checks container images for known security issues and malware.
- **Docker Security Scanning**: Integrated with Docker Hub (available on paid plans) and other third-party services that scan images for vulnerabilities.
- **Clair**: A static analysis tool for vulnerability scanning of container images.

These tools compare the software within your image against a database of known vulnerabilities, helping you catch issues early in the development lifecycle.

15.1.3 Best Practices for Image Scanning

- **Automate Scanning in CI/CD Pipelines**: Integrate vulnerability scanning into your continuous integration/continuous deployment process. This ensures that every image is scanned before it's deployed.
- **Regularly Update Base Images**: Use minimal, official, and frequently updated base images. Keep them up-to-date with security patches.
- **Review Scan Reports**: Actively monitor and address any vulnerabilities reported by the scanning tools.

15.2 Running Containers with Non-Root Users

15.2.1 The Risk of Running as Root

By default, many container images run as the **root** user. If a container is compromised, an attacker might leverage the root privileges to cause greater damage, potentially impacting the host system or other containers.

15.2.2 Best Practices for User Management

- **Create a Non-Root User**: Modify your Dockerfile to add a non-root user and switch to that user before starting the application. For example:

```dockerfile
FROM python:3.10-slim

# Create a non-root user and group
RUN groupadd -r appgroup && useradd -r -g appgroup appuser

# Set working directory
WORKDIR /app

# Copy your application code
COPY . .

# Install dependencies
RUN pip install --no-cache-dir -r requirements.txt

# Change ownership and switch user
RUN chown -R appuser:appgroup /app
USER appuser

# Define the command to run your application
CMD ["python", "app.py"]
```

- **Minimize Privileges**: Only grant the permissions necessary for your application to function.
- **Review and Harden Container Configurations**: Regularly audit your container configurations to ensure that they adhere to the principle of least privilege.

15.3 Managing Secrets Securely

15.3.1 The Importance of Secrets Management

Containers often require sensitive information—such as API keys, database passwords, and encryption keys—to operate correctly. Storing these secrets in your image or in plain text configuration files poses a significant security risk.

15.3.2 Best Practices for Secrets Management

- **Use Environment Variables Wisely**: While environment variables can pass secrets to containers, avoid hardcoding them in Dockerfiles or Compose files that are committed to version control.
- **Leverage Docker Secrets**: For Docker Swarm deployments, use Docker Secrets to manage sensitive data. This feature encrypts and manages secrets securely within the Swarm.
- **External Secret Managers**: Integrate with dedicated secret management tools such as HashiCorp Vault, AWS Secrets Manager, or Azure Key Vault to retrieve secrets at runtime.
- **Rotate Secrets Regularly**: Establish a policy for regular rotation of sensitive credentials to reduce the window of opportunity for compromised secrets.

15.4 Real-World Example: Scanning a Base Image with Trivy

To illustrate the importance of image scanning, let's walk through a real-world example using **Trivy**.

15.4.1 Step 1: Install Trivy

If you haven't installed Trivy yet, you can do so with the following command:

```bash
brew install trivy   # For macOS users using Homebrew
```

Alternatively, follow the installation instructions on the Trivy GitHub repository.

15.4.2 Step 2: Scan a Base Image

Assume you're using a minimal Python base image:

```bash
docker pull python:3.10-slim
```

Run Trivy to scan the image:

```bash
trivy image python:3.10-slim
```

Trivy will analyze the image and output a report listing any detected vulnerabilities, including details on the severity, affected packages, and suggested remediation steps.

15.4.3 Step 3: Analyze and Act on the Report

Review the scan output carefully:

- **Identify Critical Vulnerabilities**: Prioritize any vulnerabilities labeled as critical or high.

- **Update or Patch**: If vulnerabilities are found in the base image or installed packages, update the image or apply patches as needed.
- **Repeat Scanning**: Integrate Trivy into your CI/CD pipeline to automate scans for every build, ensuring no new vulnerabilities are introduced.

Conclusion

Securing containerized applications requires diligence at every layer—from the moment an image is built until a container is running in production. By scanning images for vulnerabilities, running containers with non-root users, and managing secrets securely, you create a robust defense against potential security breaches. Tools like Trivy help automate this process, catching issues before they reach production.

Implement these best practices consistently to safeguard your applications, maintain compliance with security standards, and build a trusted container ecosystem. With proactive security measures, you can confidently deploy containerized applications in any environment.

Key Takeaways

1. **Image Scanning**:
    - Regularly scan your base images with tools like Trivy or Docker Security Scanning to detect vulnerabilities and malware early.
2. **Non-Root Users**:

o Configure your Dockerfiles to create and use non-root users, minimizing potential damage if a container is compromised.

3. **Secrets Management**:
   o Avoid hardcoding sensitive data; use Docker Secrets, environment variables with care, or external secret managers to securely manage credentials.

4. **Automation in CI/CD**:
   o Integrate security scanning and automated secret management into your CI/CD pipelines for continuous protection.

5. **Real-World Example**:
   o Using Trivy to scan a Python base image demonstrates a practical approach to identifying and mitigating vulnerabilities before deployment.

CHAPTER 16

Advanced Container Security and Compliance

Introduction

While basic container security practices help safeguard everyday applications, enterprise environments and regulated industries demand a higher level of rigor. In this chapter, we examine advanced security mechanisms and compliance requirements to protect sensitive data and meet industry standards. We begin by exploring Linux security profiles—AppArmor and SELinux—that provide an extra layer of defense by enforcing granular access controls. Next, we discuss Docker security best practices tailored for regulated environments, including HIPAA and PCI-DSS, and the importance of maintaining strong container isolation in multi-tenant systems. Finally, we conclude with a real-world example that shows how to implement SELinux policies on an enterprise server hosting multiple containers.

16.1 Security Profiles: AppArmor and SELinux

16.1.1 Understanding Linux Security Modules

Linux offers robust security modules that extend standard permission systems. Two of the most prominent are:

- **AppArmor (Application Armor)**: AppArmor confines programs by enforcing access control policies that restrict file system and network operations. Its profiles are path-based and relatively easier to configure, making it popular for many containerized applications.
- **SELinux (Security-Enhanced Linux)**: SELinux enforces mandatory access controls (MAC) using a set of detailed policies based on the principle of least privilege. Unlike AppArmor, SELinux is label-based and can offer granular control over interactions between processes, files, and network resources.

16.1.2 Benefits for Container Security

Using these security profiles helps ensure that even if an attacker compromises a container, their ability to access host resources or other containers is severely limited. When applied correctly, these tools can enforce boundaries that go beyond traditional Docker isolation mechanisms.

16.2 Docker Security Best Practices for Regulated Industries

16.2.1 Compliance Considerations

Industries such as healthcare and finance face strict regulatory standards like HIPAA and PCI-DSS. Docker security best practices for these industries include:

- **Regular Vulnerability Scanning and Patch Management**:

Ensure that all base images and container dependencies are updated with the latest security patches. Automated scanning tools integrated into your CI/CD pipelines can be essential here.

- **Hardening Container Configurations**: Limit container privileges, disable unused capabilities, and enforce resource limits to reduce the risk of exploitation.
- **Audit Logging and Monitoring**: Implement logging and monitoring solutions that track container activity, access patterns, and potential security incidents. This is critical for compliance audits.
- **Encryption and Data Protection**: Encrypt sensitive data both at rest and in transit. Use secure channels for container communications and enforce strict access controls.

16.2.2 Best Practices in Action

Following industry guidelines means:

- Running containers with non-root users.
- Using minimal, trusted base images.
- Isolating sensitive workloads into dedicated networks or even separate host clusters.
- Employing robust secrets management systems to avoid hardcoding credentials in images or configuration files.

16.3 Container Isolation in Multi-Tenant Environments

16.3.1 The Challenge of Multi-Tenancy

In multi-tenant environments, multiple applications or services run on shared infrastructure. This scenario increases the risk of a security breach in one container affecting others. Therefore, proper isolation is essential.

16.3.2 Isolation Strategies

- **Namespace   Isolation**:
  Docker already leverages Linux namespaces to isolate containers; however, coupling this with security modules like SELinux further restricts interactions between containers and the host.
- **Resource   Quotas   and   Limits**:
  Apply CPU, memory, and I/O limits to ensure that no single container can consume excessive resources, which could otherwise lead to denial-of-service conditions.
- **Dedicated   Networks   and   Segmentation**:
  Use custom Docker networks to separate groups of containers. This limits the exposure of sensitive services to only those containers that need to communicate with them.
- **Security Profiles and Mandatory Access Controls**:
  Enforcing AppArmor or SELinux policies across a multi-tenant system adds a robust security layer that mitigates the risks associated with shared resources.

16.4 Real-World Example: Implementing SELinux Policies on an Enterprise Server

16.4.1 Scenario Overview

Imagine an enterprise server that hosts multiple containers running applications processing sensitive customer data. To comply with regulatory requirements, you must ensure that if one container is compromised, it cannot access data or resources beyond its designated scope.

16.4.2 Steps to Implement SELinux Policies

1. **Enable SELinux on the Host**: Ensure that your enterprise server is running SELinux in enforcing mode. You can check the status with:

bash

```
sestatus
```

2. **Define SELinux Policies for Containers**: Create or modify SELinux policy modules to restrict container interactions. For example, you can write a custom policy that only allows specific read and write operations within designated directories:

bash

```
module container_policy 1.0;

require {
    type container_t;
    type container_file_t;
    class file { read write };
}

# Allow containers to read and write only
within a specific directory
allow container_t container_file_t:file {
read write };
```

Compile and load the module:

bash

210

```
checkmodule -M -m -o container_policy.mod
container_policy.te
semodule_package -o container_policy.pp -m
container_policy.mod
semodule -i container_policy.pp
```

3. **Apply Policies to Containers**:
   Launch your containers ensuring they run with the
   appropriate SELinux context. Docker automatically
   applies default contexts, but you can customize them
   via runtime options if necessary:

```bash

docker run -d --name secure_app --security-
opt label:type:container_t my_secure_image
```

4. **Monitor and Audit**:
   Use SELinux audit logs to verify that your policies
   are effective. Examine
   `/var/log/audit/audit.log` to see if any
   unauthorized access attempts are being blocked.

16.4.3 Benefits of the SELinux Implementation

- **Enhanced Isolation**:
  The SELinux policy restricts container access to only
  the necessary file system areas, reducing the risk that
  a compromised container can interfere with others.
- **Compliance Assurance**:
  By enforcing strict access controls, the enterprise
  server is better positioned to comply with regulatory
  requirements such as HIPAA or PCI-DSS.
- **Operational Transparency**:
  SELinux audit logs provide visibility into container

operations, aiding in security audits and incident response.

Conclusion

Advanced container security and compliance are vital for enterprises handling sensitive data or operating in regulated industries. By leveraging security profiles like AppArmor and SELinux, organizations can enforce mandatory access controls that greatly reduce the attack surface. Combining these tools with Docker's best practices—such as running containers with non-root users, limiting container privileges, and managing secrets securely—provides a multi-layered defense strategy. In multi-tenant environments, these measures ensure that a breach in one container does not jeopardize the entire infrastructure.

The real-world example of implementing SELinux policies on an enterprise server demonstrates how these advanced security measures can be applied to protect sensitive data effectively. As you deploy containerized applications in complex, high-stakes environments, these strategies become essential for maintaining security, compliance, and operational integrity.

Key Takeaways

1. **Security Profiles (AppArmor, SELinux):**
   o Provide mandatory access controls that restrict container operations beyond standard Docker isolation.
2. **Regulatory Compliance:**

    o   Implement Docker security best practices to meet standards like HIPAA and PCI-DSS, including vulnerability scanning, privilege minimization, and proper secrets management.

3. **Container Isolation in Multi-Tenant Environments**:
   - Use namespaces, resource limits, dedicated networks, and SELinux/AppArmor policies to maintain strict isolation.

4. **Real-World SELinux Example**:
   - Enabling SELinux, writing custom policies, and applying them to containers on an enterprise server protects sensitive data and supports compliance.

5. **Holistic Approach**:
   - Combining advanced security measures with continuous monitoring and automated compliance checks fortifies your containerized infrastructure.

CHAPTER 17

Performance Tuning and Resource Management

Introduction

In any production environment, ensuring that your applications run efficiently is critical. Docker offers tremendous benefits by packaging applications into lightweight containers, but without proper tuning, containerized applications may not fully utilize available hardware resources—or they might even introduce unexpected overhead. In this chapter, we dive into the art and science of performance tuning in Docker. We'll discuss how to manage CPU and memory limits, examine the nature of container overhead, and explore strategies for optimizing Dockerfiles. Finally, we'll walk through a real-world example that benchmarks a high-throughput web service running inside Docker compared to a bare-metal deployment, highlighting differences in memory usage and response times.

17.1 CPU and Memory Limits

17.1.1 Why Set Resource Limits?

Containers share the host's operating system kernel, which means that if one container consumes excessive resources, it can affect others running on the same host. By setting CPU and memory limits, you ensure that each container only uses the resources allocated to it, maintaining overall system stability and performance.

17.1.2 How to Configure Limits

- **CPU   Limits**:
  Use the `--cpus` flag when running a container to restrict the number of CPU cores it can use. For example:

  bash

  ```
  docker run --cpus="1.5" myimage
  ```

  This command limits the container to 1.5 CPUs.

- **Memory   Limits**:
  Use the `-m` or `--memory` flag to set a maximum memory usage. For example:

  bash

  ```
  docker run -m 512m myimage
  ```

  This command restricts the container's memory usage to 512 megabytes.

17.1.3 Benefits of Resource Limiting

- **Stability**: Prevents a single container from monopolizing system resources.
- **Predictability**: Offers more consistent performance, particularly in multi-tenant environments.
- **Scalability**: Helps in planning capacity and scaling applications horizontally by understanding resource usage per container.

17.2.1 What Is Container Overhead?

Even though containers are lightweight compared to virtual machines, there is still some overhead associated with managing namespaces, control groups (cgroups), and networking. Understanding this overhead is essential when comparing containerized environments to bare-metal deployments.

17.2.2 Key Considerations

- **Resource   Consumption**: Containers may incur slight overhead due to the isolation mechanisms provided by Docker. This overhead is usually minimal but can become significant in highly resource-constrained environments.
- **Performance   Benchmarks**: Measuring performance (e.g., CPU cycles, memory usage, and I/O operations) in containerized environments helps identify bottlenecks and optimize resource allocation.

17.2.3 Strategies to Minimize Overhead

- **Use   Minimal   Base   Images**: Choose images like Alpine or slim variants to reduce the bloat and lower the overhead.
- **Optimize   Dockerfiles**: Each additional layer in a Docker image can contribute to increased overhead. Combining related commands into single layers reduces complexity and improves performance.

17.3 Optimizing Dockerfiles for Faster Builds and Smaller Images

17.3.1 Best Practices for Dockerfile Optimization

- **Minimize the Number of Layers**: Combine commands where possible using `&&` to reduce the number of intermediate layers.
- **Leverage Caching**: Place commands that change infrequently (e.g., installing system dependencies) near the top of the Dockerfile so that subsequent builds can use cached layers.
- **Use Slim or Alpine Variants**: Start with a minimal base image to reduce image size and build time.
- **Clean Up After Installations**: Remove temporary files and caches during the build process to keep the final image as lean as possible.

17.3.2 Example of an Optimized Dockerfile

Here's a comparison snippet showing a less optimal Dockerfile versus an optimized one:

Non-Optimized Dockerfile:

```dockerfile
FROM node:14
RUN apt-get update && apt-get install -y git
COPY . /app
RUN cd /app && npm install
CMD ["node", "/app/server.js"]
```

Optimized Dockerfile:

dockerfile

```
FROM node:14-alpine
RUN apk update && apk add --no-cache git
WORKDIR /app
COPY package.json ./
RUN npm install --production
COPY . .
CMD ["node", "server.js"]
```

Optimizations include:

- Using the Alpine version of the Node image.
- Installing packages with no cache.
- Setting a working directory to simplify subsequent commands.
- Copying only necessary files first to leverage Docker's caching mechanism.

17.4 Real-World Example: Benchmarking a High-Throughput Web Service

17.4.1 Scenario Overview

Imagine you have a high-throughput web service that processes thousands of requests per second. You want to evaluate its performance when running inside a Docker container versus on bare-metal.

17.4.2 Benchmark Setup

- **Bare-Metal   Setup**:
  Deploy the web service directly on the host without containerization. Monitor CPU usage, memory consumption, and response times under load using tools like Apache Bench (`ab`), JMeter, or similar.

- **Docker** **Setup**:
  Containerize the web service using an optimized Dockerfile. Set appropriate CPU and memory limits (e.g., `--cpus="1.5"` and `-m 512m`). Use monitoring tools such as Docker stats and Prometheus to collect performance metrics.

17.4.3 Benchmarking Process

1. **Deploy** **Both** **Environments**:
   Ensure that both the bare-metal and containerized instances are running the same version of the web service.
2. **Simulate** **Load**:
   Use a load testing tool to send a similar volume of requests to each setup.
3. **Collect Metrics**:
   - o **Memory Usage**: Compare peak and average memory usage.
   - o **CPU Utilization**: Monitor CPU load and throttling.
   - o **Response Times**: Measure average response time and request latency.
   - o **Throughput**: Analyze the number of requests handled per second.
4. **Analyze** **Overhead**:
   Compare the performance metrics to identify any additional overhead introduced by Docker. Note that while containers are lightweight, the orchestration layer and isolation mechanisms may slightly affect performance compared to a bare-metal deployment.

17.4.4 Observations and Outcomes

- **Memory** **and** **CPU** **Utilization**:
  The containerized service may use marginally more

memory due to Docker's internal processes, but proper resource limits can help mitigate this effect.

- **Response   Times**:
  Typically, response times should be very similar if the container is well-optimized, although slight latency might be observed in high-load scenarios.
- **Scalability**:
  The containerized environment often offers better scalability and manageability, enabling dynamic resource allocation and easier horizontal scaling.

Conclusion

Optimizing container performance and managing hardware resources are crucial steps in deploying high-performance, scalable applications. By setting appropriate CPU and memory limits, understanding container overhead, and optimizing Dockerfiles, you can minimize performance penalties and achieve near bare-metal performance for many applications. Our real-world benchmarking example illustrates that while Docker introduces a slight overhead, the benefits of scalability, manageability, and resource isolation often outweigh these costs.

In this chapter, you learned how to fine-tune Docker containers for performance, ensuring that they run efficiently without overburdening your hardware resources. As you incorporate these practices into your development and production workflows, you'll be better prepared to handle high-throughput applications in both containerized and non-containerized environments.

Key Takeaways

1. **Resource Limits**:
   o Use CPU and memory limits (`--cpus` and `-m`) to ensure that containers do not overconsume resources.
2. **Container Overhead**:
   o Understand the minimal overhead introduced by Docker and work to mitigate it through careful configuration.
3. **Dockerfile Optimization**:
   o Write efficient Dockerfiles by minimizing layers, leveraging caching, and using slim base images.
4. **Performance Benchmarking**:
   o Compare containerized applications with bare-metal deployments to measure the impact of containerization on memory usage, CPU utilization, and response times.
5. **Scalability and Manageability**:
   o Despite a small overhead, containers offer significant advantages in scalability and resource management that can outweigh performance differences.

CHAPTER 18

High Availability and Disaster Recovery

Introduction

In today's production environments, ensuring that your containerized applications remain available during failures or disasters is critical. High availability (HA) and disaster recovery (DR) are not just buzzwords—they are essential strategies to protect your business continuity. In this chapter, we explore various approaches to achieve resilience and rapid recovery in containerized systems. We delve into multi-region deployments that distribute workloads across different geographic areas, discuss backup and restore processes to safeguard data, and look at automated failover techniques that minimize downtime. By implementing these strategies, you can build a robust, resilient infrastructure that maintains service availability even in adverse conditions.

18.1 Multi-Region Deployments

18.1.1 The Importance of Geographic Redundancy

Deploying your applications across multiple regions or Availability Zones (AZs) ensures that if one location experiences an outage or disaster, your services can continue operating from another location. This approach reduces the risk of a single point of failure and improves overall service availability.

18.1.2 Strategies for Multi-Region Deployments

- **Cloud Provider Regions and AZs**: Leverage the multi-region architecture offered by cloud providers such as AWS, GCP, or Azure. For example, AWS organizes its infrastructure into regions and Availability Zones, enabling you to distribute containers across physically separated data centers.
- **Load Balancing and DNS**: Utilize global load balancers or DNS-based routing to direct traffic to the healthiest or nearest region. Tools like AWS Route 53 or GCP Cloud DNS can help manage failover and routing.
- **Data Replication**: Ensure that critical data is replicated across regions using cloud-native storage solutions or database replication mechanisms. This minimizes data loss and facilitates quick recovery.

18.2 Backups and Restore Processes for Containerized Databases

18.2.1 The Need for Regular Backups

Containerized databases can be highly dynamic. Regular backups are essential to protect against accidental data loss, corruption, or ransomware attacks. A well-planned backup strategy allows you to restore your data quickly and maintain business continuity.

18.2.2 Implementing Backup Processes

- **Automated Backup Scripts**: Use tools like `pg_dump` for PostgreSQL or `mysqldump` for MySQL in conjunction with cron jobs or containerized backup services. These scripts can periodically create backups of your databases.
- **Volume Snapshots and Storage Solutions**: Cloud providers offer native snapshot services for persistent storage volumes. For example, AWS EBS snapshots can capture the state of your data volumes, enabling quick restoration if needed.
- **Centralized Backup Repositories**: Store backups in a centralized, secure location such as Amazon S3, Google Cloud Storage, or a dedicated backup server. Ensure that these repositories are themselves replicated and secured.

18.2.3 Restore Processes

- **Testing Restores**: Regularly test your restore process in a staging environment to ensure that backups are valid and that recovery procedures work as expected.
- **Automated Restore Workflows**: In the event of a failure, use automation (scripts or orchestration tools) to spin up new containers, attach restored volumes, and reconfigure networking so that your services can resume normal operations quickly.

18.3 Automated Failover Techniques

18.3.1 Ensuring Rapid Recovery

Automated failover is critical to minimize downtime. Failover techniques monitor service health and automatically redirect traffic or restart services if a failure is detected.

18.3.2 Tools and Techniques

- **Health Checks and Monitoring**: Use built-in health checks (in Docker Swarm or Kubernetes) to monitor container health continuously. Orchestrators can automatically replace unhealthy containers.
- **Service Discovery and Load Balancing**: Both Docker Swarm and Kubernetes include native load balancing features. These systems automatically reroute traffic from failed containers to healthy ones.
- **Orchestration Policies**: Define policies that trigger automated scaling, container restarts, or even region failovers when certain thresholds are met. This can include rolling updates and zero-downtime deployments.

18.4 Real-World Example: Configuring a Cluster Across Multiple Availability Zones

18.4.1 Scenario Overview

Imagine you have a critical web application that needs to maintain 99.99% uptime. To achieve this, you decide to deploy your application using either Docker Swarm or Kubernetes across multiple Availability Zones on AWS. This multi-AZ setup ensures that if one AZ experiences an outage, your application remains available in the others.

18.4.2 Step-by-Step Implementation

1. **Cluster Setup**:
   - **For Docker Swarm**:
     Initialize Swarm mode on a manager node located in one AZ, and then join worker nodes from two or more additional AZs using the provided join token.

     bash

     ```
     docker swarm init --advertise-addr
     <MANAGER_IP>
     docker swarm join --token
     <WORKER_TOKEN> <MANAGER_IP>:2377
     ```

   - **For Kubernetes**:
     Use a managed service like EKS or GKE that automatically distributes nodes across multiple AZs, or manually set up a cluster ensuring nodes are placed in different zones.

2. **Deploying the Application**:
   - Convert your Docker Compose file (if using Docker Swarm) into a Swarm stack, or prepare Kubernetes manifests.
   - Deploy the stack or manifests, ensuring that your deployment specifies multiple replicas.

     bash

     ```
     docker stack deploy -c docker-compose.yml production_stack
     ```

     For Kubernetes, use:

     bash

     ```
     kubectl apply -f deployment.yaml
     kubectl apply -f service.yaml
     ```

3. **Implementing Automated Failover**:
   o **Health** **Checks**:
   Configure health checks in your deployment configuration. In Kubernetes, this might involve setting up liveness and readiness probes.
   o **Load** **Balancing**:
   Use an external load balancer (such as AWS ELB) that distributes traffic across the nodes in different AZs.
   o **Monitoring** **and** **Alerts**:
   Set up monitoring with tools like Prometheus and Grafana to track performance and alert you in case of failures.
4. **Testing Disaster Recovery**:
   o Simulate an AZ failure by temporarily stopping nodes in one Availability Zone.
   o Verify that traffic is automatically rerouted to nodes in other AZs and that the application remains responsive.
   o Test the restore process by verifying that database backups can be restored and that the application can recover its state.

18.4.3 Benefits Observed

- **Resilience**:
  The application remains available even when one or more AZs are down.
- **Reduced** **Downtime**:
  Automated failover minimizes manual intervention and reduces recovery time.
- **Improved** **Scalability**:
  The cluster can dynamically adjust resource allocation based on load across different regions.

Conclusion

Achieving high availability and effective disaster recovery in a containerized environment requires a multi-layered approach. By deploying across multiple regions or Availability Zones, implementing robust backup and restore processes, and leveraging automated failover techniques, you can significantly enhance the resilience of your applications. In this chapter, we explored strategies for distributing workloads geographically, safeguarding critical data, and ensuring rapid recovery through automation. The real-world example of configuring a Swarm or Kubernetes cluster across multiple AZs on AWS or GCP demonstrates how these practices come together to create a reliable, high-availability system.

Key Takeaways

1. **Multi-Region Deployments**:
   o Distribute your containers across multiple Availability Zones or regions to minimize the risk of complete service outages.
2. **Backup and Restore Processes**:
   o Regularly back up containerized databases and test restore procedures to ensure data integrity during disasters.
3. **Automated Failover Techniques**:
   o Use built-in health checks, load balancing, and orchestration policies to automate the recovery process.
4. **Real-World Example**:
   o Configuring a Docker Swarm or Kubernetes cluster across multiple AZs on AWS/GCP provides a practical framework for achieving high availability and disaster recovery.

5. **Comprehensive Resilience**:
   - A combination of geographic distribution, robust backup strategies, and automation ensures that your containerized applications remain resilient and recoverable under various failure scenarios.

PART V

Real-World Implementations and Use Cases

CHAPTER 19

Containerizing Legacy Applications

Introduction

Legacy applications—often developed before containerization became mainstream—present unique challenges when it comes to modernization. Many of these systems are monolithic in design, with tightly coupled components, complex dependencies, and assumptions about the underlying operating system. However, encapsulating a legacy application within a Docker container can help modernize its deployment, simplify scaling, and ease maintenance. In this chapter, we'll explore common pitfalls associated with containerizing legacy applications, discuss strategies for gradually breaking down a monolith into container-friendly services, and outline testing and rollback procedures to ensure a smooth transition. We'll conclude with a real-world example demonstrating how to encapsulate a decade-old Java or .NET application using Docker with minimal code changes.

19.1 Identifying Potential Pitfalls

19.1.1 Dependency Complexity

Legacy applications often come bundled with a host of dependencies that may not align with modern, container-friendly practices. These dependencies can include outdated libraries, hardcoded paths, or system-specific binaries that assume a particular operating system version.

- **Tip**: Inventory the application's dependencies and check for compatibility with the base image you plan to use. Use tools such as dependency managers or static analysis to uncover potential conflicts.

19.1.2 OS-Level Constraints

Many legacy applications are built with the assumption that they run on a full operating system, sometimes requiring administrative privileges or specific system configurations.

- **Tip**: Evaluate the application's reliance on OS-specific features. Where possible, replace direct system calls with container-compatible alternatives or adjust the container's configuration (e.g., through privileged mode, if absolutely necessary) while keeping security in mind.

19.1.3 Configuration and Environment Coupling

Older systems may assume that configuration files and runtime environments are in fixed locations. This tight coupling can complicate the containerization process, where a more ephemeral, dynamic environment is expected.

- **Tip**: Consider externalizing configuration data using environment variables, volumes, or configuration management tools to decouple the application from its underlying environment.

19.2 Breaking Down a Monolith into Container-Friendly Services

19.2.1 The "Containerize First" Approach

For many legacy applications, the first step is to encapsulate the entire monolith in a Docker container. This "lift and shift" approach minimizes changes to the application while gaining immediate benefits such as consistent deployment and easier scaling.

- **Tip**: Start by writing a Dockerfile that mirrors the legacy environment as closely as possible. Use an appropriate base image (e.g., a Java or .NET runtime) to minimize the need for extensive modifications.

19.2.2 Incremental Decomposition

Once the application is containerized, consider a gradual refactoring process to break the monolith into smaller, container-friendly services. Techniques like the Strangler Fig pattern allow you to incrementally replace parts of the monolith without a complete overhaul.

- **Tip**: Identify discrete components or modules that can function independently, and containerize them as separate services. Use inter-container communication (via Docker networks) to maintain functionality during the transition.

19.3 Testing and Rollback Strategies

19.3.1 Comprehensive Testing

Before fully migrating a legacy application into production containers, rigorous testing is essential.

- **Integration Testing**: Validate that the containerized application interacts correctly with external systems.
- **Performance Testing**: Benchmark the container's performance against the legacy deployment to identify any bottlenecks.
- **Security Testing**: Ensure that the containerized environment does not inadvertently expose vulnerabilities.

19.3.2 Rollback Procedures

Given the complexities of legacy systems, it's critical to plan for rollback if issues arise.

- **Versioned Images**: Tag Docker images with version numbers so that you can quickly revert to a known stable state.
- **Blue/Green Deployments**: Use deployment strategies that allow you to switch traffic between the legacy (blue) and containerized (green) versions seamlessly.
- **Automated Scripts**: Develop automation to back up current configurations and restore previous versions if necessary.

19.4 Real-World Example: Containerizing a Legacy Java/.NET Application

Imagine a decade-old Java or .NET application that has been running on dedicated hardware for years. The application has a complex dependency tree and is tightly coupled to its host operating system. Here's how you might containerize it with minimal code changes:

19.4.1 Step 1: Create a Dockerfile

For a legacy Java application:

dockerfile

```
# Use an official Java runtime as the base image
FROM openjdk:8-jre-alpine

# Set the working directory
WORKDIR /app

# Copy the application JAR file into the
container
COPY legacy-app.jar /app/legacy-app.jar

# Expose the required port (e.g., 8080)
EXPOSE 8080

# Run the application with minimal changes
CMD ["java", "-jar", "legacy-app.jar"]
```

For a legacy .NET application:

dockerfile

```
# Use the official .NET runtime as the base image
FROM mcr.microsoft.com/dotnet/aspnet:3.1

# Set the working directory
WORKDIR /app

# Copy the application files into the container
COPY . /app

# Expose the port the application listens on
EXPOSE 5000

# Start the application with minimal
modifications
ENTRYPOINT ["dotnet", "LegacyApp.dll"]
```

19.4.2 Step 2: Build and Run the Container

Build the image:

```bash
docker build -t legacy-app:1.0 .
```

Run the container:

```bash
docker run -d -p 8080:8080 --name legacy-app legacy-app:1.0
```

19.4.3 Step 3: Test and Monitor

- **Testing**: Access the application via the published port to ensure it behaves as expected.
- **Monitoring**: Use Docker logs and monitoring tools to verify that resource usage and performance are within acceptable limits.

19.4.4 Step 4: Rollback Strategy

If issues are detected:

- Use the version tag to quickly revert:

  ```bash
  docker run -d -p 8080:8080 --name legacy-app-rollback legacy-app:<previous-version>
  ```

- Leverage blue/green deployment practices to switch traffic back to the previous stable version.

Conclusion

Containerizing legacy applications is a critical step in modernizing IT infrastructure, allowing organizations to leverage the benefits of Docker—consistent deployment, scalability, and simplified management—without a complete rewrite of existing systems. By identifying potential pitfalls, employing a "containerize first" strategy, and planning for incremental decomposition, you can transition legacy applications into a containerized environment smoothly. Furthermore, robust testing and rollback strategies ensure that any issues can be quickly addressed, minimizing disruption.

The real-world example demonstrates that even complex, decade-old applications can be encapsulated in Docker containers with minimal changes to the codebase, providing a pathway to modernization while preserving functionality.

Key Takeaways

1. **Identify Pitfalls**:
   - Legacy applications often have complex dependencies and OS level constraints that require careful planning before containerization.
2. **Containerize First, Then Refactor**:
   - Start by encapsulating the entire monolith in a container, then gradually break it down into smaller, container-friendly services.
3. **Testing and Rollback**:
   - Implement thorough testing and maintain versioned images to ensure a safe rollback if issues arise.
4. **Real-World Application**:

- o Minimal code changes can enable a legacy Java or .NET application to run inside a container, facilitating easier deployment and future scalability.

5. **Incremental Modernization**:
    - o Use the container as a stepping stone toward a microservices architecture, enabling a phased transition from a monolith to a modern, scalable application design.

CHAPTER 20

Building a Microservices Architecture with Docker

Introduction

Modern application development is rapidly moving toward the microservices architecture—a design pattern in which an application is broken down into a collection of small, loosely coupled, independently deployable services. Docker plays a vital role in this paradigm by providing a lightweight, consistent, and scalable way to package and run each microservice in isolation.

In this chapter, we will explore the core principles of microservices, examine how different services communicate (via REST APIs, gRPC, or message queues), and discuss strategies for deploying and scaling each service independently. To bring these concepts to life, we will walk through a real-world example of a simplified e-commerce application where the user, product, and order services are containerized separately, allowing for independent development, deployment, and scaling.

20.1 Core Principles of Microservices

20.1.1 Decentralization and Independence

Microservices are designed to be autonomous. Each service is responsible for a specific business capability and is developed, deployed, and scaled independently. This decentralization allows teams to work in parallel, adopt different technology stacks, and iterate quickly without waiting on a monolithic release cycle.

20.1.2 Single Responsibility

Each microservice is built around a single, well-defined purpose. For instance, in an e-commerce application, one service might handle user authentication, another manages product listings, and yet another processes orders. This separation of concerns makes the system easier to understand and maintain.

20.1.3 Resilience and Scalability

Microservices are designed to be resilient. If one service fails, it does not necessarily bring down the entire system. Additionally, services can be scaled independently based on their workload. For example, if the order service experiences heavy traffic during a sale, it can be scaled out without scaling the user or product services.

20.2 Communication Between Services

20.2.1 REST APIs

Many microservices communicate using HTTP-based REST APIs. This approach is straightforward and leverages standard web protocols for interoperability. Each service exposes a set of endpoints that other services can consume.

20.2.2 gRPC

For scenarios that require high-performance, low-latency communication, gRPC offers a robust solution. gRPC uses HTTP/2, supports streaming, and allows for strict interface contracts via Protocol Buffers.

20.2.3 Message Queues

Message queues, such as RabbitMQ or Apache Kafka, enable asynchronous communication between services. This decoupling ensures that services can process tasks at their own pace, improving resilience and allowing for smoother load distribution.

20.3 Deployment and Scaling Each Service Independently

20.3.1 Containerization and Isolation

Docker allows each microservice to run in its own container, ensuring that its dependencies, runtime, and configuration are isolated from other services. This isolation prevents conflicts and simplifies both development and deployment.

20.3.2 Independent Scaling

With Docker, you can deploy multiple replicas of a particular service to handle increased load without affecting other services. Orchestrators like Docker Swarm, Kubernetes, or Docker Compose enable you to manage scaling policies, ensuring that services can automatically scale up or down as needed.

20.3.3 Continuous Deployment

Containerization facilitates continuous integration and continuous deployment (CI/CD) pipelines. Since each microservice is packaged as a Docker image, updating a service involves building a new image and redeploying that container, all while other services continue running uninterrupted.

20.4 Real-World Example: A Simplified E-Commerce Application

Imagine a simplified e-commerce platform that consists of three key microservices:

1. **User Service**: Handles user registration, authentication, and profile management.
2. **Product Service**: Manages product listings, details, and inventory.
3. **Order Service**: Processes orders, tracks order status, and manages transactions.

20.4.1 Service Breakdown

- **User Service**:
  - **Technology**: Could be built using Node.js or Python.
  - **Endpoints**: `/register`, `/login`, `/profile`.
  - **Container**: Packaged into its own Docker container with a dedicated database or connection to a centralized user datastore.
- **Product Service**:

- **Technology**: Could be built with Java, .NET, or any language suitable for handling data-intensive tasks.
- **Endpoints**: `/products`, `/products/{id}`, `/inventory`.
- **Container**: Runs in its own container, possibly connecting to a separate NoSQL or SQL database.

- **Order Service**:
  - **Technology**: Developed in Go or another performant language.
  - **Endpoints**: `/orders`, `/orders/{id}`, `/order-history`.
  - **Container**: Encapsulated in a container that may communicate asynchronously with other services via message queues.

20.4.2 Inter-Service Communication

- **User Service and Order Service** might communicate over REST APIs to verify user credentials and fetch user details.
- **Order Service** can use a message queue (like RabbitMQ) to trigger inventory updates in the **Product Service** asynchronously.
- **Product Service** exposes a REST API that both the **User Service** and **Order Service** can consume to retrieve product details.

20.4.3 Deployment Example Using Docker Compose

A simplified `docker-compose.yml` for this microservice system might look like this:

```yaml
version: '3.9'
```

```
services:
  user-service:
    image: user-service:latest
    ports:
      - "5001:5001"
    environment:
      - SERVICE_PORT=5001
    networks:
      - ecommerce-net

  product-service:
    image: product-service:latest
    ports:
      - "5002:5002"
    environment:
      - SERVICE_PORT=5002
    networks:
      - ecommerce-net

  order-service:
    image: order-service:latest
    ports:
      - "5003:5003"
    environment:
      - SERVICE_PORT=5003
    networks:
      - ecommerce-net

networks:
  ecommerce-net:
    driver: bridge
```

In this configuration:

- Each microservice runs in its own container.
- Services are connected through a custom bridge network (ecommerce-net), enabling them to discover and communicate with each other using their container names.
- Ports are published to allow external access, and environment variables configure service-specific settings.

20.4.4 Scaling and Independent Deployment

Using an orchestration platform like Docker Swarm or Kubernetes, you can scale each service independently based on demand. For example:

- If the order service becomes a bottleneck during a sale, you can scale it to five replicas while keeping the user and product services at their current capacity.
- Updates to a single service can be deployed without redeploying the entire application, enabling continuous delivery practices.

Conclusion

Docker is a powerful enabler of the microservices paradigm. By containerizing individual services, you can achieve greater isolation, independent scaling, and more robust inter-service communication. In this chapter, we explored the core principles of microservices, various communication mechanisms (REST, gRPC, message queues), and strategies for deploying and scaling each service independently. Our real-world example of a simplified e-commerce application illustrated how a microservices architecture can be built, managed, and scaled using Docker containers, paving the way for agile development and continuous improvement.

Key Takeaways

1. **Core Principles of Microservices**:
   o Microservices are decentralized, single-purpose, and designed for resilience and independent scaling.

2. **Inter-Service Communication**:
   o Services can interact via REST APIs, gRPC, or asynchronous message queues, depending on performance and complexity requirements.
3. **Deployment and Scaling**:
   o Docker enables each service to be deployed and scaled independently, offering flexibility and fault isolation.
4. **Real-World Application**:
   o A simplified e-commerce platform with user, product, and order services demonstrates how Docker supports a microservices architecture.
5. **Benefits**:
   o Faster development cycles, easier maintenance, and enhanced scalability are among the significant advantages of using Docker for microservices.

CHAPTER 21

CI/CD with Docker

Introduction

In modern software development, rapid, reliable, and repeatable deployments are critical. Continuous Integration and Continuous Deployment (CI/CD) pipelines streamline the process of building, testing, and deploying applications. When combined with Docker, these pipelines ensure that every stage—from local development to production—is consistent and isolated. This chapter shows you how to integrate Docker into your CI/CD workflow using popular tools like GitLab CI/CD, GitHub Actions, or Jenkins. We also examine how Docker-based testing environments can replicate production conditions and describe deployment strategies that allow for zero-downtime rollouts, such as blue-green and rolling updates.

21.1 Creating a CI/CD Pipeline

21.1.1 Overview

A CI/CD pipeline automates the sequence of steps required to build, test, and deploy your application. Integrating Docker into this process provides several benefits:

- **Consistency**: Docker images encapsulate your environment, ensuring that the same configuration is used in development, testing, and production.

- **Isolation**: Each pipeline stage runs in its own container, reducing conflicts between dependencies.
- **Speed**: Automated builds and tests reduce manual intervention and accelerate feedback loops.

21.1.2 Pipeline Tools

Several CI/CD platforms support Docker integration, including:

- **GitLab CI/CD**: Offers native Docker support with runners that can build and run containers.
- **GitHub Actions**: Provides workflows that can use Docker containers for testing and deployment.
- **Jenkins**: With Docker plugins, Jenkins can spin up containers for builds and tests.

21.1.3 Example Pipeline Snippet (GitHub Actions)

Below is a simplified example of a GitHub Actions workflow that builds a Docker image and runs tests:

```yaml
yaml

name: CI/CD Pipeline

on:
  push:
    branches: [ main ]
  pull_request:
    branches: [ main ]

jobs:
  build:
    runs-on: ubuntu-latest

    steps:
    - name: Checkout code
      uses: actions/checkout@v2
```

248

```
- name: Build Docker image
  run: |
    docker build -t myapp:latest .

- name: Run tests inside container
  run: |
    docker run --rm myapp:latest npm test

- name: Push image to registry
  if: github.ref == 'refs/heads/main'
  run: |
    docker      login        -u       ${{
secrets.DOCKER_USERNAME   }}      -p       ${{
secrets.DOCKER_PASSWORD }}
    docker         tag          myapp:latest
myregistry.com/myapp:latest
    docker push myregistry.com/myapp:latest
```

This workflow demonstrates key steps:

- **Checkout**: Pull the code from the repository.
- **Build**: Create a Docker image.
- **Test**: Run tests inside a temporary container.
- **Push**: Authenticate and push the image to a Docker registry if the commit is on the main branch.

21.2 Docker-Based Testing Environments

21.2.1 Advantages

Using Docker for testing ensures that the test environment mirrors the production environment as closely as possible. This reduces the "it works on my machine" problem by:

- **Isolating Dependencies**: Each test runs in a container with exactly the dependencies specified in your Dockerfile.

- **Replicability**: The same image can be used for local tests, CI/CD pipelines, and production deployments.

21.2.2 Implementation

For a Node.js/React application:

- **Unit and Integration Tests**: Use a containerized environment to run tests with frameworks like Jest (for JavaScript) or Mocha.
- **End-to-End Testing**: Set up containers to simulate a full stack (e.g., web server, database) and run tests that mimic real user interactions.

21.3 Zero-Downtime Deployments

21.3.1 Blue-Green Deployments

Blue-green deployments involve maintaining two identical production environments:

- **Blue**: The currently running version.
- **Green**: The new version to be deployed.

Traffic is switched from blue to green after thorough testing, ensuring minimal downtime.

21.3.2 Rolling Updates

Rolling updates gradually replace instances of the old version with new ones. This method allows a portion of the service to remain available at all times, reducing service interruptions.

21.3.3 Automation in Orchestrators

Orchestration platforms like Docker Swarm or Kubernetes support these deployment strategies natively, making it easier to implement zero-downtime updates:

- **Swarm**: Use service update commands with rolling update options.
- **Kubernetes**: Configure Deployments with rolling update strategies and readiness/liveness probes.

21.4 Real-World Example: Full Pipeline for a Node.js/React Application

21.4.1 Scenario Overview

Consider a Node.js/React e-commerce application that requires frequent updates and automated testing. The CI/CD pipeline for this application will:

1. **Build Docker Images**: Package the Node.js backend and React frontend into Docker images.
2. **Run Tests**: Execute unit and integration tests inside Docker containers.
3. **Push to Registry**: Store the built images in a Docker registry.
4. **Deploy to Staging**: Automatically deploy the updated images to a staging environment for further testing.
5. **Auto-Deploy to Production**: After successful staging tests, roll out the update to production using blue-green or rolling update strategies.

21.4.2 Pipeline Breakdown

1. **Build Stage**:
   o Build separate Docker images for the backend and frontend using optimized Dockerfiles.

o   Example command:

```bash
docker build -t mybackend:latest
./backend
docker build -t myfrontend:latest
./frontend
```

2. Test Stage:
o   Run automated tests in containers:

```bash
docker run --rm mybackend:latest npm
test
docker run --rm myfrontend:latest
npm test
```

3. Push Stage:
o   Tag and push the images:

```bash
docker tag mybackend:latest
myregistry.com/mybackend:latest
docker push
myregistry.com/mybackend:latest
docker tag myfrontend:latest
myregistry.com/myfrontend:latest
docker push
myregistry.com/myfrontend:latest
```

4. Deployment Stage (Staging):
o   Use a deployment tool (e.g., Docker Swarm, Kubernetes, or even Docker Compose) to deploy the images to a staging environment.
o   Monitor the application and run integration tests.

5. Deployment Stage (Production):

    o   Use blue-green or rolling updates to deploy the images to production, ensuring zero downtime.

    o   For example, in Kubernetes, update the Deployment resource with the new image tag and let Kubernetes handle the rolling update.

21.4.3 Orchestration Example

Using Kubernetes, you might have a deployment manifest for the backend like:

```yaml
apiVersion: apps/v1
kind: Deployment
metadata:
  name: backend-deployment
spec:
  replicas: 3
  selector:
    matchLabels:
      app: backend
  strategy:
    type: RollingUpdate
    rollingUpdate:
      maxUnavailable: 1
      maxSurge: 1
  template:
    metadata:
      labels:
        app: backend
    spec:
      containers:
      - name: backend
        image: myregistry.com/mybackend:latest
        ports:
        - containerPort: 3000
```

This manifest specifies:

- A rolling update strategy with controlled surge and unavailability.
- The new image is pulled automatically when the Deployment is updated.

Conclusion

Integrating Docker into a CI/CD pipeline brings consistency, speed, and reliability to your development lifecycle. By automating builds, tests, and deployments, you reduce manual errors and ensure that every change is validated in an environment that mirrors production. Whether you use GitLab CI/CD, GitHub Actions, Jenkins, or another tool, Docker-based pipelines simplify the process of continuous delivery. With strategies like blue-green and rolling updates, you can achieve zero-downtime deployments, ensuring a smooth user experience even during updates.

The real-world example of a Node.js/React application demonstrates how a comprehensive CI/CD pipeline can be implemented—from building and testing Docker images to deploying them through staging and production environments. This approach not only accelerates the development process but also enhances the overall reliability and scalability of your applications.

Key Takeaways

1. **CI/CD Integration**:
   o Docker streamlines the automation of building, testing, and deploying applications.
2. **Pipeline Tools**:

- o Tools such as GitLab CI/CD, GitHub Actions, and Jenkins can seamlessly integrate Docker into your workflows.

3. **Docker-Based Testing**:
   - o Consistent containerized testing environments reduce discrepancies between development and production.

4. **Zero-Downtime Deployments**:
   - o Blue-green and rolling update strategies enable smooth transitions during updates.

5. **Real-World Example**:
   - o A full pipeline for a Node.js/React application shows how automated builds, tests, and deployments can be achieved, leading to faster iterations and increased reliability.

CHAPTER 22

Docker for Data Science and Machine Learning

Introduction

In the rapidly evolving field of data science and machine learning, reproducibility, scalability, and portability are crucial. Docker offers a solution that encapsulates the entire runtime environment—dependencies, libraries, and configurations—into a single container. This not only ensures that your code behaves the same way across different environments but also simplifies sharing and deployment. In this chapter, we explain how Docker can be used to package Python and R environments, leverage GPU acceleration for deep learning, and manage versioning of both data and models. By the end, you'll see a practical example of Dockerizing a Jupyter Notebook environment tailored for machine learning experiments.

22.1 Packaging Python and R Environments

22.1.1 Encapsulating Dependencies

Data science projects often require a complex set of libraries and tools. Docker makes it easy to package these dependencies together:

256

- **Python Environments**: Whether using `pip` or Conda, you can define all necessary packages in a Dockerfile or an environment file. This approach guarantees that everyone on your team uses the same package versions.
- **R Environments**: Similarly, R-based workflows can be containerized by installing CRAN or Bioconductor packages into a Docker image. This isolation prevents conflicts with system-level libraries.

22.1.2 Example Dockerfile for a Python Environment

Below is an example Dockerfile that uses a Python base image, installs Conda (or directly uses pip), and sets up a reproducible environment for data science:

```dockerfile
FROM python:3.9-slim

# Install system dependencies
RUN apt-get update && apt-get install -y --no-install-recommends \
    build-essential \
    && rm -rf /var/lib/apt/lists/*

# Copy the requirements file and install Python packages
COPY requirements.txt /app/requirements.txt
WORKDIR /app
RUN pip install --no-cache-dir -r requirements.txt

# Expose a port for Jupyter Notebook (if needed)
EXPOSE 8888

# Default command (this can be overridden)
CMD ["python"]
```

In this Dockerfile, `requirements.txt` lists all your Python packages, ensuring that the environment is identical on every build.

22.2 GPU Support in Docker for Deep Learning Tasks

22.2.1 Leveraging GPU Acceleration

Deep learning tasks often require GPU acceleration to dramatically reduce training and inference times. Docker can access GPUs via Nvidia-Docker, which allows containers to use the host's GPU hardware.

22.2.2 Enabling GPU Access

- **Nvidia-Docker**:
  Install Nvidia-Docker (or the newer Nvidia Container Toolkit) on your host. When running a container, use the `--gpus` flag:

  ```bash
  docker run --gpus all -it my-deep-learning-image
  ```

- **Selecting the Right Base Image**:
  Use Nvidia's CUDA base images (e.g., `nvidia/cuda:11.2.0-runtime`) to ensure compatibility with GPU drivers and libraries required by frameworks like TensorFlow or PyTorch.

22.3 Versioning Data and Models

22.3.1 Reproducibility in ML

Versioning is critical for reproducibility in machine learning:

- **Data Versioning**: Tools such as DVC (Data Version Control) can track changes in datasets, ensuring that models are trained on the correct data versions.
- **Model Versioning**: Tag your Docker images with specific model versions (e.g., `my-model:v1.0`, `my-model:v2.0`). This allows you to easily revert or compare different iterations.

22.3.2 Integrating with CI/CD

Automate the versioning process by integrating your Docker build and deployment pipeline with CI/CD tools. Every time you update your data or model, a new Docker image can be automatically built and pushed to a registry, ensuring traceability.

22.4 Real-World Example: Dockerizing a Jupyter Notebook Environment

Imagine a data science team that needs a reproducible environment for running machine learning experiments. They decide to Dockerize a Jupyter Notebook environment pre-configured with libraries such as TensorFlow and PyTorch.

22.4.1 Creating the Dockerfile

Below is an example Dockerfile for setting up a Jupyter Notebook environment:

```dockerfile
FROM python:3.9-slim

# Install system dependencies and GPU support
libraries if needed
RUN apt-get update && apt-get install -y --no-
install-recommends \
    build-essential \
    && rm -rf /var/lib/apt/lists/*

# Install Jupyter and common ML libraries
RUN pip install --no-cache-dir jupyter tensorflow
torch torchvision pandas scikit-learn matplotlib

# Create a working directory
WORKDIR /notebooks

# Expose port 8888 for Jupyter Notebook
EXPOSE 8888

# Start Jupyter Notebook
CMD ["jupyter", "notebook", "--ip=0.0.0.0", "--
port=8888", "--no-browser", "--allow-root"]
```

22.4.2 Building and Running the Container

Build the Docker image:

```bash
docker build -t ml-notebook:latest .
```

Run the container (with GPU support if available):

```bash
```

260

```
docker   run   --gpus   all   -p   8888:8888   -v
$(pwd)/notebooks:/notebooks ml-notebook:latest
```

This command maps the container's `/notebooks` directory to a local folder, enabling you to persist and share your notebooks.

22.4.3 Benefits for Reproducible ML Experiments

- **Consistency**: Every team member uses the same Docker image, ensuring that experiments are reproducible.
- **Portability**: The entire environment can be run on any machine with Docker and Nvidia-Docker installed.
- **Collaboration**: Changes to the environment (e.g., library updates) are controlled via versioned Dockerfiles and integrated into CI/CD pipelines.

Conclusion

Docker is an invaluable tool for data scientists and machine learning practitioners. By encapsulating complex environments into portable containers, Docker ensures that your ML experiments are reproducible, scalable, and easy to share. Whether you are packaging a Python or R environment, enabling GPU acceleration for deep learning, or managing versioned datasets and models, Docker streamlines the entire process. The real-world example of Dockerizing a Jupyter Notebook environment highlights how these benefits come together to facilitate efficient and collaborative ML workflows.

Key Takeaways

1. **Packaging Environments**:
   o Docker can package Python and R environments, ensuring that all dependencies are consistently installed across different systems.
2. **GPU Support**:
   o With Nvidia-Docker, Docker containers can leverage GPU acceleration for deep learning tasks, significantly improving performance.
3. **Versioning**:
   o Effective versioning of data and models within Docker images promotes reproducibility and easier rollback if necessary.
4. **Real-World Application**:
   o Dockerizing a Jupyter Notebook environment pre-configured with ML libraries like TensorFlow and PyTorch enables reproducible experiments and smooth team collaboration.
5. **Collaborative Workflows**:
   o Integrating Docker into your CI/CD pipeline ensures that every update to your ML environment is automated, traceable, and consistent across development, testing, and production.

CHAPTER 23

Managing State and Databases with Docker

Introduction

Containers are often celebrated for their ability to package applications in an isolated, ephemeral environment. However, when it comes to stateful services—such as databases—the very nature of containers poses a challenge. Data stored inside a container can be lost if the container is stopped, restarted, or redeployed. This chapter explores best practices for running databases in Docker, handling backups and upgrades safely, and managing stateful containers in orchestrated environments. We will also demonstrate a production-grade MongoDB replicaset as a real-world example of how to manage stateful services effectively.

23.1 Running Relational and NoSQL Databases in Containers

23.1.1 Relational Databases

Containers can run relational databases like MySQL and PostgreSQL effectively if you follow certain guidelines:

- **Persistence**: Use Docker volumes to persist data outside the container's lifecycle. This ensures that even if the container is removed, your data remains intact.

- **Configuration**: Externalize configuration and secrets (like passwords) using environment variables or Docker secrets.
- **Resource Allocation**: Limit CPU and memory resources to prevent a database container from consuming too many host resources.

23.1.2 NoSQL Databases

NoSQL databases such as MongoDB and Redis are also popular choices in containerized environments:

- **Data Replication**: Many NoSQL systems support replication and sharding. Running a replicaset (for MongoDB) or a cluster (for Redis) improves availability and scalability.
- **Network Configuration**: Ensure that containers are placed on a common network so that they can discover and communicate with each other.
- **State Management**: Use volumes to store data and maintain state across container restarts and updates.

23.2 Handling Backups and Upgrades

23.2.1 Backup Strategies

For both relational and NoSQL databases, regular backups are crucial:

- **Volume Snapshots**: Use Docker volumes in conjunction with cloud provider snapshot features (like AWS EBS snapshots) to capture data periodically.
- **Database-Specific Tools**: Utilize native backup tools (e.g., `mysqldump` for MySQL, `pg_dump` for PostgreSQL, or `mongodump` for MongoDB) within a container to create data backups.

- **Automated Jobs**: Schedule backup tasks using cron jobs inside a container or as part of your orchestration platform's job scheduler.

23.2.2 Upgrade Strategies

Upgrading stateful services requires careful planning:

- **Versioned Deployments**: Always tag your database images with version numbers, so you can roll back if an upgrade causes issues.
- **Blue/Green Deployments**: Deploy a new version in parallel with the existing one, then gradually switch traffic once the new version is verified.
- **Data Migration**: Ensure that schema migrations and data transformations are tested thoroughly before deploying to production.

23.3 Stateful Containers in Orchestrated Environments

23.3.1 Orchestration with Kubernetes StatefulSets

Kubernetes provides a special construct known as a **StatefulSet** for managing stateful applications:

- **Stable Identity**: Each pod in a StatefulSet has a stable network identity and persistent storage.
- **Ordered Deployment and Scaling**: Pods are created, updated, or scaled in a predictable order, which is critical for databases that require coordination between nodes.
- **Persistent Volume Claims (PVCs)**: Automatically provision persistent storage that is tied to the lifecycle of the pod, ensuring data is retained even if a pod is rescheduled.

23.3.2 Docker Swarm Considerations

While Docker Swarm does not have a native equivalent to Kubernetes StatefulSets, you can still run stateful applications by:

- **Using Named Volumes**: Explicitly define and mount named volumes to maintain data persistence.
- **Service Constraints**: Configure service placement to ensure that stateful containers are distributed appropriately and can access the required storage.

23.4 Real-World Example: Production-Grade MongoDB Replicaset

Imagine you need to deploy a MongoDB replicaset to ensure high availability and data redundancy. Below is an outline of how you can achieve this using Docker Swarm or Kubernetes.

23.4.1 Setting Up the Environment

1. **Define Persistent Storage**: Create a Docker named volume (or Kubernetes PersistentVolume) to store MongoDB data:

   bash

   ```
   docker volume create mongo-data
   ```

   In Kubernetes, you would define a PersistentVolume and a PersistentVolumeClaim.

2. **Deploying a Replicaset in Docker Swarm**:
   o **Initialize Swarm**:

   bash

```
docker swarm init
```

o **Deploy MongoDB Service**: Create a service with multiple replicas and ensure each replica uses the persistent volume. You may need to configure the MongoDB replicaset settings via environment variables or initialization scripts. An example `docker-compose.yml` for Swarm might include:

```yaml
version: '3.9'
services:
  mongo:
    image: mongo:4.4
    volumes:
      - mongo-data:/data/db
    environment:
      -
MONGO_INITDB_REPLICA_SET_NAME=rs0
    deploy:
      replicas: 3
    networks:
      - mongo-net

volumes:
  mongo-data:

networks:
  mongo-net:
    driver: overlay
```

Then deploy with:

```bash
docker stack deploy -c docker-compose.yml mongo-stack
```

267

o **Initialize the Replicaset**:
Once the containers are running, connect to one instance and initiate the replicaset configuration using the Mongo shell:

```bash
docker exec -it <mongo_container_id>
mongo
> rs.initiate()
> rs.add("mongo:27017")
```

Adjust the commands as necessary to include all replica members.

3. **Deploying a Replicaset in Kubernetes**:
   o **StatefulSet Manifest**:
   Create a StatefulSet YAML file for MongoDB. A simplified version might look like:

```yaml
apiVersion: apps/v1
kind: StatefulSet
metadata:
  name: mongo
spec:
  serviceName: "mongo"
  replicas: 3
  selector:
    matchLabels:
      app: mongo
  template:
    metadata:
      labels:
        app: mongo
    spec:
      containers:
      - name: mongo
        image: mongo:4.4
        ports:
```

```
        - containerPort: 27017
        volumeMounts:
        - name: mongo-storage
          mountPath: /data/db
        env:
        -                              name:
MONGO_INITDB_REPLICA_SET_NAME
            value: "rs0"
    volumeClaimTemplates:
    - metadata:
        name: mongo-storage
      spec:
        accessModes: [ "ReadWriteOnce"
]
        resources:
          requests:
            storage: 10Gi
```

Apply the manifest using:

```
bash
```

```
kubectl      apply      -f      mongo-
statefulset.yaml
```

o **Initialize   the   Replicaset**:
Similar to Swarm, use the Mongo shell to
configure the replicaset:

```
bash
```

```
kubectl exec -it mongo-0 -- mongo
> rs.initiate()
> rs.add("mongo-1.mongo:27017")
> rs.add("mongo-2.mongo:27017")
```

23.4.2 Benefits Observed

- **High   Availability**:
  The replicaset ensures that if one node fails, the remaining
  nodes continue to serve data.

- **Data   Redundancy**:
  Multiple replicas mean that data is stored redundantly, reducing the risk of data loss.
- **Scalability**:
  Orchestrated environments allow for easy scaling of the replicaset and seamless integration with monitoring and backup systems.

Conclusion

Running stateful services and databases in Docker requires careful planning and adherence to best practices. By using persistent storage, handling backups and upgrades properly, and leveraging orchestrated environments like Kubernetes StatefulSets or Docker Swarm with named volumes, you can achieve a robust, production-grade setup. The real-world example of deploying a MongoDB replicaset demonstrates that with the right configuration, containerized databases can meet the high availability, redundancy, and scalability demands of modern applications.

Key Takeaways

1. **Stateful Services in Containers**:
   o Use Docker volumes or Kubernetes PersistentVolumeClaims to maintain data persistence for databases.
2. **Database Best Practices**:
   o Follow guidelines for both relational and NoSQL databases to ensure consistent performance and security.
3. **Backup and Upgrade Strategies**:
   o Implement regular backups and carefully plan upgrades to minimize downtime and data loss.

4. **Orchestrated Environments**:
   o Use Kubernetes StatefulSets or Docker Swarm services with named volumes to manage stateful containers.
5. **Real-World Example**:
   o Deploying a MongoDB replicaset across multiple nodes ensures high availability and data redundancy, critical for production-grade applications.

CHAPTER 24

Case Studies: Enterprise Docker Success Stories

Introduction

As organizations continue to modernize their IT infrastructures, many have turned to Docker for its promise of consistency, scalability, and agility. This chapter showcases several enterprise success stories that demonstrate Docker's real-world impact across various industries. Whether in finance, healthcare, media, or e-commerce, Docker has enabled companies to streamline deployments, reduce infrastructure costs, and improve operational resilience. We will explore the implementation details, lessons learned, and challenges encountered by these organizations. In particular, we will take a close look at a bank's journey toward adopting Docker—focusing on the compliance and security hurdles they overcame to achieve faster deployment cycles and cost savings.

24.1 Industry Examples: Diverse Success Stories

24.1.1 Finance

Financial institutions have stringent security and compliance requirements. Several banks and investment firms have adopted Docker to standardize their deployment processes, isolate critical services, and maintain robust audit trails. By containerizing legacy applications and integrating with CI/CD pipelines, these organizations have reduced deployment times from days to minutes, while ensuring that sensitive financial data is protected and regulatory requirements are met.

24.1.2 Healthcare

In healthcare, ensuring patient data privacy and meeting regulatory standards like HIPAA is paramount. Hospitals and healthcare providers have used Docker to deploy microservices architectures that isolate patient data processing, facilitate secure data sharing, and improve scalability. Containerization has enabled healthcare organizations to integrate advanced analytics and telemedicine services without compromising on data security or system reliability.

24.1.3 Media

Media companies often require rapid scalability to handle unpredictable traffic spikes—such as during live broadcasts or major events. By adopting Docker, media enterprises have been able to deploy scalable, containerized streaming platforms and content management systems. These platforms can automatically scale based on demand, ensuring smooth viewer experiences even during peak load times.

24.1.4 E-commerce

E-commerce businesses benefit from Docker's ability to modularize applications, allowing each service (e.g., user authentication, product catalog, shopping cart, and order processing) to be deployed and scaled independently. This modularity has resulted in more resilient architectures and faster feature iterations. Additionally, Docker's portability enables e-commerce platforms to run consistently across on-premises and cloud environments, reducing the risks associated with migrations and scaling.

24.2.1 Standardizing Deployment with Docker

One of the primary benefits noted across these industries is the ability to standardize deployments. By creating container images that encapsulate application dependencies and configurations, enterprises eliminate the "works on my machine" problem. A consistent environment across development, testing, and production has led to:

- **Reduced Deployment Times**: Automated pipelines and container orchestration allow organizations to deploy updates rapidly.
- **Simplified Rollbacks**: Versioned Docker images make it easy to revert to a previous state in the event of issues.
- **Streamlined Compliance Audits**: Immutable images provide a verifiable record of the software in production, simplifying audits and compliance reporting.

24.2.2 Overcoming Legacy System Challenges

Many enterprises face the daunting task of modernizing legacy applications. The case studies reveal that:

- **Containerization Is Often a Gradual Process**: A "lift and shift" strategy can encapsulate a monolithic legacy application into a container with minimal code changes.

274

Over time, organizations can refactor and decompose the application into microservices.

- **Interoperability is Key**: Successful deployments required careful integration with existing monitoring, logging, and security systems. This often meant extending Docker's native capabilities with third-party tools.
- **Training and Culture Shift**: Adopting Docker frequently involves a cultural shift. Investing in training and developing clear documentation proved essential for teams to transition smoothly to a containerized workflow.

24.3 Common Challenges and How They Were Overcome

24.3.1 Security and Compliance

Enterprises in highly regulated industries initially struggled with container security. Overcoming these challenges required:

- **Integrating Security Scanning Tools**: Automated image scanning and runtime security monitoring were implemented to ensure compliance with regulatory standards.
- **Using Docker Secrets and External Secret Managers**: Sensitive information was handled more securely, reducing risks associated with hardcoded credentials.
- **Implementing Strict Access Controls**: Running containers with non-root users and enforcing robust network policies helped maintain strict isolation between services.

24.3.2 Performance and Scalability

Scaling containerized applications to meet high traffic demands required fine-tuning:

- **Resource Management**: CPU and memory limits were set to prevent any single container from affecting overall performance.
- **Optimizing Dockerfiles**: Lean base images and multi-stage builds were adopted to reduce image sizes and speed up deployment.
- **Leveraging Orchestration**: Tools like Docker Swarm and Kubernetes provided automated load balancing and scaling, ensuring that applications remained responsive even under heavy load.

24.4 Real-World Example: A Bank's Adoption of Docker

24.4.1 Background

A mid-sized bank, facing mounting pressure to reduce IT costs and accelerate deployment cycles, embarked on a modernization project. The bank had several legacy applications running on traditional servers, and the slow, manual deployment processes were hindering its ability to innovate. Additionally, stringent compliance and security requirements meant that any new technology had to integrate seamlessly with existing security frameworks.

24.4.2 Implementation

The bank's journey with Docker began with a pilot project:

- **Containerization of Legacy Applications**: A decade-old Java application was encapsulated in Docker containers with minimal code modifications. The focus was on preserving functionality while modernizing the deployment process.
- **Automated CI/CD Pipeline**: Docker was integrated into the bank's CI/CD pipeline using Jenkins. Automated

builds, tests, and deployments reduced manual errors and accelerated release cycles.

- **Security Enhancements**: Docker images were scanned regularly using security tools such as Trivy. The bank also implemented Docker secrets and ran containers as non-root users to comply with regulatory standards.
- **Compliance and Audit Readiness**: Immutable images and versioned deployments provided a clear audit trail, easing the compliance reporting process.

24.4.3 Results and Lessons Learned

- **Cost Savings**: The bank reported significant reductions in infrastructure and operational costs due to improved resource utilization and streamlined deployment processes.
- **Faster Deployment Cycles**: Deployment times dropped from weeks to mere hours, allowing for more frequent updates and faster response to market demands.
- **Enhanced Security and Compliance**: Automated scanning and strict access controls ensured that the bank maintained compliance with financial regulations such as PCI-DSS and SOX.
- **Cultural Shift**: A key lesson was the importance of training and collaboration across IT and development teams. Overcoming initial resistance led to a more agile and innovative environment.

Conclusion

Real-world success stories demonstrate that Docker can transform enterprise IT operations across a wide range of industries. From finance to healthcare, media to e-commerce, containerization has enabled organizations to deploy applications faster, reduce costs, and meet stringent compliance requirements. The bank's journey serves as a compelling example of how legacy systems can be modernized through Docker, overcoming challenges in security, performance, and cultural adoption.

By understanding these case studies and lessons learned, readers are better equipped to apply Docker in their own enterprises—whether it's through containerizing legacy applications, integrating CI/CD pipelines, or architecting scalable microservices.

Key Takeaways

1. **Diverse Industry Applications**:
   o Enterprises in finance, healthcare, media, and e-commerce have successfully adopted Docker to solve unique challenges.
2. **Standardization and Efficiency**:
   o Docker enables consistent, automated deployments that reduce costs and accelerate time-to-market.
3. **Overcoming Legacy Challenges**:
   o Containerizing legacy applications is often a gradual process that starts with a lift-and-shift approach, followed by incremental refactoring.
4. **Security and Compliance**:
   o Implementing robust security measures (image scanning, non-root containers, Docker secrets) is critical for regulated industries.
5. **Real-World Inspiration**:
   o A bank's successful Docker adoption illustrates how Docker can deliver cost savings, faster deployments, and improved compliance, inspiring other enterprises to follow suit.

PART VI

Advanced Topics and Looking Ahead

CHAPTER 25

Monitoring and Logging in Docker Environments

Introduction

In a containerized world, maintaining visibility into your applications is crucial for ensuring reliability, diagnosing issues, and optimizing performance. Unlike traditional applications, Docker environments are inherently dynamic: containers can start, stop, and scale rapidly. To effectively manage such an environment, you need a robust observability strategy. This chapter introduces key tools and practices for centralized logging, metrics collection, and health monitoring, enabling you to keep a pulse on your Dockerized applications in real time.

25.1 Centralized Logging

25.1.1 Why Centralized Logging?

Centralized logging collects logs from multiple containers into a single repository where they can be stored, searched, and analyzed. This approach is essential for troubleshooting, auditing, and gaining insights into application behavior.

25.1.2 Popular Logging Solutions

- **ELK Stack (Elasticsearch, Logstash, Kibana)**:
  - o **Elasticsearch** indexes and stores logs.
  - o **Logstash** collects and processes log data from various sources.
  - o **Kibana** provides a visual interface for querying and analyzing logs.
- **Splunk**:
  - o A commercial solution offering robust log analysis, real-time monitoring, and alerting capabilities.
- **Fluentd/Fluent Bit**:
  - o Open-source log collectors that can forward logs to various backends including Elasticsearch and Splunk.

25.1.3 Best Practices

- **Standardize Log Format**: Use JSON or another structured format to simplify parsing and analysis.
- **Configure Log Rotation**: Prevent disk space issues by setting up log rotation policies.
- **Secure Log Transmission**: Encrypt logs in transit to protect sensitive data.

25.2 Metrics Collection

25.2.1 The Importance of Metrics

Collecting performance metrics allows you to monitor resource usage (CPU, memory, network), track application performance, and detect anomalies before they escalate into issues.

25.2.2 Popular Metrics Solutions

- **Prometheus**:

- o An open-source system for monitoring and alerting that collects and stores time-series data.
- **Grafana**:
  - o A visualization tool that works seamlessly with Prometheus to create detailed dashboards.
- **Other Tools**:
  - o Alternatives like Datadog or New Relic offer integrated monitoring solutions for containerized environments.

25.2.3 Best Practices

- **Define Key Performance Indicators (KPIs)**: Identify metrics that matter to your application, such as response times, error rates, and resource utilization.
- **Set Up Alerts**: Use threshold-based alerts to notify you when metrics exceed predefined limits.
- **Automate Data Collection**: Instrument your applications to expose metrics endpoints, and ensure that your monitoring system scrapes these endpoints at regular intervals.

25.3 Health Checks and Container-Level Monitoring

25.3.1 Health Checks

Health checks are crucial for detecting and isolating failing containers. Docker supports both built-in health checks (specified in a Dockerfile) and external monitoring solutions.

- **Docker Health Checks**:
  - o Define a health check command in your Dockerfile to periodically test the container's health.
  - o Example:

```
dockerfile

HEALTHCHECK     --interval=30s     --
timeout=5s     CMD     curl     -f
http://localhost:8080/health || exit
1
```

- **External Monitoring**:
  - o Use tools like Prometheus and Grafana to monitor health metrics and container status.

25.3.2 Container-Level Monitoring

Monitoring containers at the individual level helps detect issues such as memory leaks, CPU spikes, or network latency.

- **Docker Stats**:
  - o Use the `docker stats` command to view real-time metrics for running containers.
- **Integration with Monitoring Tools**:
  - o Tools like Prometheus Node Exporter can gather detailed metrics from Docker hosts, providing a comprehensive view of container performance.

25.4   Real-World   Example: Implementing   an
Observability Stack

25.4.1 Scenario Overview

Consider a microservices-based application deployed via Docker. The application comprises several containers, including web services, databases, and caching layers. To ensure smooth operations, you need a complete observability stack that captures logs, aggregates metrics, and monitors container health—alerting you when issues arise.

25.4.2 Implementation Steps

1. **Set Up Centralized Logging with the ELK Stack**:
   - **Elasticsearch**: Deploy an Elasticsearch container to store logs.
   - **Logstash/Fluentd**: Configure Logstash or Fluentd to collect logs from your Docker containers (using a logging driver or sidecar container) and forward them to Elasticsearch.
   - **Kibana**: Deploy a Kibana container to visualize and analyze logs.
   - *Example*:

```yaml
version: '3.9'
services:
  elasticsearch:
    image:
docker.elastic.co/elasticsearch/ela
sticsearch:7.10.0
    environment:
      - discovery.type=single-node
    ports:
      - "9200:9200"
  logstash:
    image:
docker.elastic.co/logstash/logstash
:7.10.0
    ports:
      - "5000:5000"
    volumes:
      -
./logstash.conf:/usr/share/logstash
/pipeline/logstash.conf
  kibana:
```

```
image:
docker.elastic.co/kibana/kibana:7.1
0.0
    ports:
      - "5601:5601"
```

- o Configure your containers to use a logging driver (e.g., Fluentd or JSON-file) that directs logs to Logstash.

2. **Collect Metrics with Prometheus and Grafana**:
   - o Deploy Prometheus to scrape metrics from your Docker host and application endpoints.
   - o Deploy Grafana to create dashboards based on Prometheus data.
   - o *Example* Prometheus configuration might include job definitions for scraping container metrics via cAdvisor or Node Exporter.

3. **Implement Health Checks and Alerting**:
   - o Define health check commands in your Dockerfiles.
   - o Configure Prometheus alerting rules to trigger alerts (e.g., when a container is marked unhealthy or when resource usage exceeds limits).
   - o Set up Grafana alerts or integrate with a notification system (such as Slack or PagerDuty).

25.4.3 Outcome

Once the observability stack is in place:

- **Centralized Logging**: All container logs are aggregated in Elasticsearch, making troubleshooting efficient.
- **Metrics Collection**: Prometheus collects real-time performance data, while Grafana dashboards provide actionable insights.
- **Health Monitoring**: Automated health checks and alerting ensure that issues are identified and addressed promptly, minimizing downtime.

Conclusion

Effective monitoring and logging are the cornerstones of maintaining healthy, high-performing containerized environments. By implementing centralized logging, robust metrics collection, and comprehensive health checks, you gain deep visibility into your Dockerized applications. The real-world example demonstrates how a complete observability stack—using tools like the ELK stack, Prometheus, and Grafana—can be deployed to monitor a set of microservices, ensuring that issues are detected early and addressed swiftly.

As your container deployments grow in complexity, these observability practices will become essential for maintaining reliability, optimizing performance, and reducing downtime.

Key Takeaways

1. **Centralized Logging**:
   o Use tools like the ELK stack or Splunk to collect, store, and analyze logs from multiple containers.
2. **Metrics Collection**:
   o Implement Prometheus and Grafana for real-time monitoring of container performance and resource usage.
3. **Health Checks**:
   o Define and monitor container health with built-in Docker health checks and external monitoring tools.
4. **Real-World Implementation**:

o A comprehensive observability stack provides centralized logs, performance metrics, and alerts, enabling proactive issue resolution.

5. **Proactive Management**:
   o Proper monitoring and logging practices ensure that your containerized applications remain resilient and performant even as they scale.

CHAPTER 26

The Docker Ecosystem and Third-Party Tools

Introduction

Docker's core technology has spawned an extensive ecosystem of tools and services that extend its capabilities, simplify management, and integrate containerization into various environments. In this chapter, we examine key components of this ecosystem, including alternative container runtimes, image management solutions, and cloud-native container platforms. We will compare Docker Desktop, Docker Engine, and Podman, discuss third-party tools such as Harbor and Portainer for image management, and review cloud-native solutions like AWS ECS, Azure Container Instances, and Google Cloud Run. Finally, we illustrate these concepts with a real-world example of migrating a Docker-based application to AWS ECS, discussing the associated cost and performance trade-offs.

26.1 Docker Desktop vs. Docker Engine vs. Podman

Docker Desktop

- **Overview**:
  Docker Desktop is an all-in-one application designed for Windows and macOS users. It packages the Docker Engine, Docker CLI, and an integrated GUI, making it

easy for developers to build, test, and run containers on their local machines.

- **Pros**:
    - o User-friendly interface and integrated tools
    - o Seamless updates and built-in support for Kubernetes (in recent versions)
- **Cons**:
    - o Limited to Windows and macOS
    - o Can be resource-intensive compared to a lean Docker Engine on Linux

Docker Engine

- **Overview**:
  Docker Engine is the core container runtime that runs on Linux servers. It handles container lifecycle management and is the backbone of many production systems.
- **Pros**:
    - o High performance and efficient resource usage on Linux
    - o Robust, mature, and widely adopted
- **Cons**:
    - o Requires familiarity with command-line tools for management
    - o Not natively available on Windows or macOS without additional virtualization layers

Podman

- **Overview**:
  Podman is an alternative, daemonless container engine that emphasizes security by supporting rootless container operations. It offers a Docker-compatible CLI and can run and manage containers without a central daemon.
- **Pros**:
    - o Enhanced security with rootless mode
    - o Docker CLI-compatible, making migration easier
- **Cons**:

- o Some differences in behavior may require minor adjustments in workflows
- o Ecosystem and community support are growing but not as mature as Docker's

26.2 Tools for Image Management

Harbor

- **Overview**:
  Harbor is an open-source container registry that enhances Docker Hub's capabilities by providing features like role-based access control (RBAC), vulnerability scanning, and image replication.
- **Benefits**:
  - o Improved security through image signing and vulnerability analysis
  - o Advanced access control and auditing, ideal for enterprise environments

Portainer

- **Overview**:
  Portainer is a lightweight management UI that provides a graphical interface to manage Docker environments. It simplifies container orchestration, image management, and network configuration.
- **Benefits**:
  - o Intuitive visual management of containers, volumes, and networks
  - o Supports Docker, Docker Swarm, and Kubernetes environments

26.3 Cloud-Native Solutions

AWS ECS (Elastic Container Service)

- **Overview**:
  AWS ECS is a fully managed container orchestration service that supports Docker containers. It can run containers on EC2 instances or using Fargate for a serverless compute model.
- **Pros**:
  - Deep integration with AWS services and security features
  - Flexible deployment options: manage your own EC2 cluster or use Fargate
- **Cons**:
  - Can be complex for smaller projects or teams new to AWS

Azure Container Instances (ACI)

- **Overview**:
  ACI provides a serverless container hosting solution on Azure. It allows you to run containers without managing underlying infrastructure.
- **Pros**:
  - Fast startup times and simplified scaling
  - Billing based on actual resource usage, which can reduce costs for bursty workloads

Google Cloud Run

- **Overview**:
  Cloud Run is a fully managed compute platform that automatically scales stateless containers. It offers a serverless experience and supports any language or library.
- **Pros**:

o Scales to zero when not in use, reducing idle costs
o Simplified deployment and integration with Google Cloud's ecosystem

26.4 Real-World Example: Migrating a Docker-Based Application to AWS ECS

26.4.1 Scenario Overview

Imagine you have a Docker-based web application that runs smoothly on your local machine using Docker Desktop. To improve scalability and integrate with enterprise cloud infrastructure, you decide to migrate the application to AWS ECS. The goal is to achieve a production-ready environment with minimal refactoring while evaluating the cost and performance trade-offs.

26.4.2 Migration Process

1. **Preparation**:
   o **Containerize the Application**: Ensure that your application is fully containerized with a well-optimized Dockerfile. Tag your image appropriately (e.g., myapp:latest).
   o **Push to a Registry**: Push your Docker image to a container registry (such as AWS ECR):

   bash

   ```
   docker        tag        myapp:latest
   aws_account_id.dkr.ecr.region.amazo
   naws.com/myapp:latest
   docker                         push
   aws_account_id.dkr.ecr.region.amazo
   naws.com/myapp:latest
   ```

2. **Set Up an ECS Cluster**:
   o **Using Fargate or EC2**: Decide whether to use the serverless Fargate launch type (which abstracts away server management) or manage your own EC2 cluster for potentially better performance control.
   o **Create a Task Definition**: Define your container specifications in an ECS task definition, including resource allocations (CPU and memory limits), environment variables, and port mappings.
   o **Deploy the Service**: Use the ECS console or CLI to create a service based on your task definition and deploy it across your cluster.
3. **Evaluating Cost and Performance Trade-offs**:
   o **Cost Considerations**:
     ▪ **Fargate**: Charges based on resource usage per second; ideal for variable workloads but can be costlier for steady, high-volume applications.
     ▪ **EC2**: May offer lower costs at scale if you optimize instance usage, but requires more management effort.
   o **Performance Considerations**:
     ▪ Monitor resource utilization and application responsiveness.
     ▪ Use AWS CloudWatch to collect metrics and set up alarms for performance thresholds.
     ▪ Compare latency and throughput with your local Docker environment to identify any discrepancies.

26.4.3 Outcome

- **Minimal Refactoring**: By leveraging a containerized application that adheres to best practices, the migration required little to no changes in the application code.

- **Improved** **Scalability**: AWS ECS enabled auto-scaling based on load, providing a robust production environment.
- **Cost** **Efficiency**: Depending on your chosen deployment mode (Fargate vs. EC2), you observed different cost dynamics, allowing you to adjust resource allocations and optimize expenses.
- **Enhanced** **Integration**: The migration facilitated better integration with other AWS services (e.g., CloudWatch for monitoring, IAM for security), streamlining the overall operations.

Conclusion

The Docker ecosystem extends far beyond the core Docker Engine. By exploring alternatives like Docker Desktop and Podman, leveraging third-party tools such as Harbor and Portainer, and tapping into cloud-native solutions like AWS ECS, Azure Container Instances, and Google Cloud Run, you can choose the best tools for your specific needs. Our real-world example of migrating a Docker-based application to AWS ECS illustrates that with minimal refactoring, you can achieve a scalable, cost-efficient, and high-performance production environment while understanding the trade-offs involved.

Key Takeaways

1. **Alternative Container Runtimes**:
   o Docker Desktop provides an all-in-one solution for local development, while Docker Engine is

the backbone for Linux deployments and Podman offers a daemonless, rootless alternative.

2. **Image Management Tools**:
   o Tools like Harbor and Portainer simplify image storage, vulnerability scanning, and overall container management.

3. **Cloud-Native Solutions**:
   o AWS ECS, Azure Container Instances, and Google Cloud Run offer managed, scalable options for deploying containerized applications in the cloud.

4. **Migration Example**:
   o Migrating a Docker-based application to AWS ECS demonstrates that with minimal code changes, enterprises can harness cloud-native benefits while carefully balancing cost and performance trade-offs.

5. **Ecosystem Flexibility**:
   o The broader Docker ecosystem provides a range of tools to fit different environments and needs, empowering organizations to build, manage, and scale containerized applications efficiently.

CHAPTER 27

The Future of Docker and Containerization

Introduction

As we reach the end of our journey through the world of Docker and containerization, it's clear that this technology has revolutionized how we build, deploy, and manage applications. Looking ahead, container technology is poised to continue evolving and influencing the broader landscape of software development and operations. In this chapter, we explore emerging trends such as serverless computing and edge computing, discuss the evolving standards that are shaping container interoperability, and offer predictions for Docker's role in future DevOps practices. We conclude with a real-world example that demonstrates how containers can empower cutting-edge AI and IoT applications at the network's edge.

27.1 Emerging Trends

27.1.1 Serverless Architectures

The serverless model is gaining traction as organizations seek to eliminate the overhead of managing infrastructure while focusing solely on code and functionality. With serverless container platforms, you can run containers without worrying about underlying servers, automatically scaling resources in response to demand. This approach enables faster development cycles and cost savings, particularly for bursty or unpredictable workloads.

27.1.2 Edge Computing

Edge computing brings processing closer to where data is generated, reducing latency and bandwidth use. Containers are ideally suited for edge computing because they are lightweight, portable, and quick to deploy. As IoT devices, distributed sensors, and autonomous systems proliferate, containerized applications at the edge will play a crucial role in processing data in real time, enabling rapid decision-making without relying on distant data centers.

27.2 Evolving Container Standards

27.2.1 The Open Container Initiative (OCI)

The Open Container Initiative (OCI) is a collaborative effort to develop open standards for container formats and runtimes. By promoting interoperability and standardization across different container technologies, OCI helps ensure that container images and runtime environments remain compatible regardless of the underlying platform. This standardization is essential for the future growth of container ecosystems, as it fosters innovation and reduces vendor lock-in.

27.2.2 Implications for the Ecosystem

As container standards continue to mature, we can expect smoother transitions between different container runtimes and orchestration systems. This evolution will benefit organizations by providing greater flexibility in choosing the best tools for their needs, whether they are deploying on-premises, in the cloud, or at the edge.

27.3 Predictions for Docker's Role in DevOps and Beyond

27.3.1 Enhanced Integration with CI/CD

Docker has already transformed DevOps by streamlining build, test, and deployment processes. Looking ahead, Docker's integration with continuous integration and continuous deployment (CI/CD) pipelines will only deepen. Automated, container-based workflows will become even more sophisticated, enabling faster iterations, improved testing environments, and more resilient deployments.

27.3.2 Expanding Use Cases

As organizations adopt more agile and distributed architectures, Docker's role will extend beyond traditional applications:

- **Hybrid Deployments**: Docker will continue to bridge on-premises and cloud environments, making it easier to deploy applications consistently across varied infrastructures.
- **Edge and IoT Applications**: Containers will become a standard tool for deploying AI models and data processing applications at the edge, supporting emerging use cases such as autonomous vehicles and smart cities.
- **Microservices and Beyond**: While Docker already underpins microservices architectures, its capabilities will

298

expand to support even more granular and dynamic service deployments, further enhancing scalability and fault tolerance.

27.4 Real-World Example: Containers at the Edge for AI and IoT

Imagine a next-generation autonomous vehicle system that relies on a network of distributed sensors and onboard AI for real-time decision-making. In such a system, latency is critical—decisions must be made in milliseconds to ensure safety and efficiency.

27.4.1 The Use Case

- **Application   Scenario**:
  A fleet of self-driving cars is equipped with sensors that continuously capture data from the environment. This data is processed by AI models running in containers deployed on edge computing nodes— either directly in the vehicles or in nearby roadside units.
- **Container   Benefits**:
  Containers allow these AI models to be updated seamlessly and deployed across diverse hardware platforms. The portability of containers ensures that the same environment used during development is also used in the field, guaranteeing consistency and reliability.

27.4.2 Implementation Details

- **Edge   Deployment**:
  Containers are deployed on small, powerful edge

servers that are located close to the vehicles. These servers handle tasks such as object detection, traffic analysis, and real-time route optimization.

- **Integration with Cloud Services**: While critical processing happens at the edge, aggregated data and model updates are synchronized with central cloud servers using container orchestration tools that support hybrid deployments.
- **Performance and Scalability**: The system can scale dynamically—deploying additional container instances on edge nodes during high-traffic periods or in response to specific events (e.g., adverse weather conditions). This elasticity is crucial for maintaining high performance and safety.

27.4.3 Outcome

This cutting-edge application demonstrates how containers can extend beyond traditional data centers to power innovative, latency-sensitive applications at the edge. By leveraging Docker's portability and standardization, the autonomous vehicle system achieves consistent performance, rapid updates, and high reliability—key factors in its success.

Conclusion

The future of Docker and containerization is both exciting and transformative. Emerging trends like serverless architectures and edge computing promise to redefine how we deploy and manage applications, while evolving container standards ensure continued interoperability and innovation. Docker's role in DevOps will only deepen, with enhanced CI/CD integration and expanded use cases that span from traditional microservices to cutting-edge AI and IoT applications. As illustrated by our real-world example, containers are set to become a foundational technology at the edge, powering advanced systems such as self-driving cars and distributed sensor networks.

As you move forward, embrace these emerging trends and leverage the strengths of Docker to build resilient, scalable, and future-ready applications.

Key Takeaways

1. **Emerging Trends**:
   o Serverless and edge computing are set to reshape container deployment, bringing processing closer to data sources and reducing latency.
2. **Evolving Standards**:
   o Initiatives like the Open Container Initiative ensure that container formats and runtimes remain interoperable, fostering innovation.
3. **Future Predictions**:
   o Docker will continue to integrate deeply with CI/CD pipelines and expand its role in hybrid and edge deployments, enabling more agile and distributed architectures.
4. **Real-World Application**:
   o Cutting-edge AI or IoT applications, such as autonomous vehicle systems, can harness containers at the edge to deliver rapid, reliable processing.
5. **Looking Ahead**:
   o The continued evolution of container technology promises to further simplify application development and operations, ensuring that Docker remains a critical tool in the DevOps toolkit.